THE FRIEND WHO STAYS

Brenda Leigh

Book Dedication

I would like to dedicate this book to my mother, Ruth Martin, and two of her sisters, my aunts, Louise Cox and Alma Gardner. Each of their first names are represented in this book in their honor by characters with just a little of their uniqueness. These three Christian ladies made a tremendous impact on my life. It truly takes a village to raise children, and God must be smiling and proud of the job all three of you did.

Table of Contents

Chapter One

Jenny Reynolds paused for a moment before knocking on the door, a nervous feeling in the pit of her stomach. There was no sound from inside the house and she couldn't help wondering what kind of mood her dad would be in today. Looking back over her shoulder, dark clouds in the west were fast approaching. She could hear thunder in the distance and knew rain would arrive soon making the need to get pans under the most recent leaks inside the house more urgent with each passing second.

Her eyes wander around the old porch noticing how obvious the house needed a painting job. The vibrant green and red of her grandmother's running roses on both sides of the porch helped hide some of the needed repairs. The rose bushes were one of the last reminders of the care the home place had once received. Her grandparents were both dead now, gone before learning that their son, her father, had been injured in combat in Afghanistan months ago where he had lost a foot. Dave Reynolds had been home for a few weeks, but the man she knew as her father was no longer there. Instead, an angry man had returned in his place, and she had no idea how to reach him.

Closing her eyes to the tears she would not let fall she pounded on the door harder this time shouting out, "Dad! It's me Jenny!" Pausing for a moment she added, "Let me in!"

"Go away," said a gruff male voice from the other side of the door. For some unknown reason the story of the *Three Little Pigs* popped into her head, but she wasn't the big bad wolf, and her dad was certainly not a little pig. She knew he was standing on the other side of the door but the distance between them may as well have been a million miles. It certainly seemed that way to her as she waited to see what her dad would do next.

"Let me in! I'm not leaving until I do what I came to do," she said still not sure if he would open the door. Finally, she heard the lock turn, and the door swung partway open, and then the sound of her father hobbling away. By the time she was able to shift the box she carried and opened the screen door, her father was disappearing into the kitchen at the end of the hallway.

As she moved toward the kitchen, she couldn't help but notice the house was in disarray just like the last time she had come by. She drew a weary sigh seeing all the bottles, cans, and dishes in the living room. Plates with old food left on them at least indicated he was eating something. Newspapers and magazines were strewn around on the floor near his recliner. By the time she reached the kitchen, her father was leaving by the back door going out toward the barn. It was like he couldn't stand to be in the same room as her. As she entered the kitchen the smell of burnt food had her wanting to hold her nose. Looking over at the stove, it took little imagination to know where the unpleasant odor came from. Opening windows in the kitchen would help, but first, she had to gather up several large plastic buckets and pans to take upstairs to place under the most recent leaks. The ceilings in two of the bedrooms were going to have to be replaced when her father finally received money from the government. Mold and mildew were taking over and she was glad her grandmother could not see the disrepair the house was in.

After placing buckets and pans under the leaks she cleaned up the mess in the kitchen. As she worked, she turned the radio on the K-Love station and sang along. After putting her father's favorite meal of roast, carrots and potatoes in the oven to cook, she went back to cleaning the kitchen. Singing along with a Casting Crown's song on the radio her heart lifted, and her mood relaxed. "Living He loved me… Dying He saved me… Buried He carried my sins far away… Rising He justified… Freely forever… One day He's coming… Oh glorious day… Oh glorious day…"

By the time the song was over, there were tears in her eyes as she looked around the room remembering all the times her grandmother had sung songs of praise as she worked. She was always telling everyone when you are down and out, singing praises to the Lord would lift your soul. She could hear her grandmother soft voice saying, "Why do you think we have those beautiful songs written by David in Psalm? Get your *Bible* out and read some of them."

Jenny found the need to pray. *Thank You, Lord. For whom shall I fear when You are here for me? I'm not sure where that is in Psalm, but I know those were words of David talking to You long ago. Thank You for giving me grandparents who told me about You. I miss them so. I pray Dad will be okay soon and if he could just find his way back to You, Lord, I know he'll get better. Please watch over Mom wherever she is, Lord. Keep her safe. Most of all thank You for Miss Ruth, without her I would be homeless. Amen*

She started a load of laundry before getting a garbage bag for the mess in the living room. It didn't take long to dispose of it and to restack the magazines on an end table beside her father's chair. The bottles and cans were placed in recycling bins to be recycled. She thought servicemen and women learned how to pick up and clean up after themselves but from the looks of the house, her father hadn't learned that lesson. Then again maybe he was rebelling and taking some time off for all the years everything had to be spotless and in its place.

The rain came down in a heavy downpour, but it didn't last long. Once it was over the rain continued to drip from the ceiling in the bedrooms. When the dripping stopped, she poured out the water and set buckets and pans back under the leaks just in case there was another shower, and she didn't get back over to take care of it. She opened all the windows upstairs and down while she finished cleaning. The fresh air was doing wonders to the smell in the house and the breeze felt cool enough to leave the windows up.

She stood back and let her gaze take in the clean kitchen. The oak cabinets were still in good shape, the wood had not lost its luster. The wallpaper was another story, the fading patterns could not be fixed. There was no hope for the once white linoleum on the floor. Even after being mopped, it didn't look much better. The apple printed curtains hanging at the windows on the east side of the house and receiving the morning sun were almost completely faded out. The curtain over the back door still held the color it was when her grandmother had hung it years before.

"Oh Grandmother, how I wish you were still here." Jenny said out loud. "You would know what to do."

The house was finally looking good again and the sun was shining by the time she started to leave. She would not be able to scout any of her cotton fields but knew she would need to check on them in case it hadn't rained there. Putting the trash in the garbage can she walked to the mailbox and pulled down the door. The box was completely full. As she glanced through mostly junk, she realized there were two from the Department of Veterans Affairs. There was one from her grandparents' insurance company and two utility bills. They were addressed to her father, but he didn't seem to be able to take care of his own business. She walked back to the house and put the mail on the table still debating what she should do. A couple of the envelopes looked as though there were checks inside. Did she get in the jeep and leave, or did she confront him about what was going on? As she walked back into the living room, she noticed mail lying under the table beside his chair. When she looked through it there were three more envelopes from the Department of Veterans Affairs but none of them had been opened?

As she went back to the kitchen still debating what she should do, she saw her father coming out of the barn heading toward the house. At least he would have a good lunch if he ate it. Maybe someday he would become the father she remembered before a decade of fighting in a war that had taken him from his family. And they were a family back then. Her mother had left shortly after her father's last deployment, and no one knew where she was. Jenny knew he wouldn't be here now if he hadn't been wounded and his career over.

Quickly looking through the rest of the mail she took out the ones that looked important and laid them on top of the other mail on the corner of the table. There were several bank statements unopened as well. Going to the cabinet she took down plates and got out silverware for two. In two glasses she poured iced tea. When the back door opened, she turned and smiled at him. He didn't smile back but at least he made eye contact. He had a questioning look on his face that asked, you are still here. She decided to ignore the look.

"You timed that just right. Everything's ready and I was just setting the table. Wash up and we can eat and talk at the same time." She didn't know what she expected but he walked into the laundry room off the kitchen, and she could hear water running in the sink.

She fixed their plates and set them on the table. Taking a chair across from her father, she waited patiently to see what he would do.

When he sat down, she was surprised when he bowed his head as if saying a blessing. After a short silence, he raised his head and reached for his fork. She knew that the roast was tender, and the potatoes and carrots were cooked just right.

After several minutes of silence, he said, "This is good. Your grandmother had to teach you because I know your mother didn't. She never could boil water without scorching it." His comment made her smile. It had been so long since he'd made the effort to share a normal conversation with her, she couldn't help the joy she felt.

"Yes, Grandma taught me," she said proudly.

"She taught you well." He paused and looked over at the mail sitting on the table.

"Dad, I think you need to open your mail," Jenny said not sure how he might take her giving him advice.

"Most of its just junk," he said without picking any of it up.

"I removed the junk mail, and you need to check the stack by your plate. Especially the utility bills and there are five government ones there too," Jenny added.

"They're just notices of what they have deposited in my bank account," he said. "Didn't you know they direct deposit everything now? The utilities are set up on an automatic payment plan."

"No, I didn't realize that."

"I'm surprised you didn't open them and look."

"Dad, I can't just open your mail."

"Your mother would have opened them and spend any money she found by now."

Jenny looked at him not sure what to say. Finally, she said, "Dad, Mom's not here anymore and I'm not her."

"Then you can take care of it for me." Dave leaned back in his chair. "Would you get me another helping?"

Pleased he was eating, she stood and took his plate to the stove and put more roast, potatoes and carrots on it. After placing the plate in front of him, she refilled his tea glass before sitting back down. He passed the mail over to her.

"Open it."

"You sure?" she said looking over at him and he gave her a nod to continue.

The first two were statements just like he had said showing how much had been deposited in his bank account. The last envelope from the Department of Defense had a check inside. She passed it across the table for him to see. As she watched him, she noticed he didn't really react to the amount.

"Dad, did you know you were getting that check?" Jenny asked.

"Yeah, they told me before I left the hospital, I would be getting some money. Not much though when you consider …," he started but stopped and looked at her as if he wasn't sure she would understand.

"What are you going to do with all that money?"

"Maybe fix the roof," he said. "Then you won't have to run over to put buckets and pans under the leaks every time you turn around."

"I don't mind coming over. But it would be great to get the roof fixed."

"Perhaps the old place could use a little work."

"You sure?" she asked. There was nothing that she would like better than to see the old home place look like it did before. Then her stomach knotted with nerves. Should she tell him? *Would he want to fix the old place up if he knew they might lose it? It wasn't fair they might spend part of his money on the house and then lose it. How could she tell him right now? This was the most her father had acted like himself since he had been home. What would he say when she finally told him? Not today. This was the first honest conversation they'd had, and she just couldn't bring herself to destroy the moment.*

"I am absolutely sure this place needs a little work," he replied.

"There is just one thing." Jenny told him.

"What's that?"

"We can get someone to fix the roof and the ceilings, but I think we can do the other work ourselves." Jenny watched for her father's reaction and was pleased when he seemed okay with that.

He hesitated for a short period of time before saying, "I may not be much help."

"You know what Grandmother would say," Jenny answered. "Start off slow and take a step at a time, don't get ahead of yourself. I know we can do this."

"When will you have time to work on it?" Her father asked.

"I can come over in the afternoons when I finish scouting the McCall's cotton fields. They trained me to go into the fields and check for insects, especially boll weevils that can damage the cotton crop. I turn in a report to the County Extension office. They look at the data and inform the farmer if and when their cotton fields need to be sprayed," Jenny answered glad she did not tell him they might lose the farm.

"Make a list of things you want us to fix, and I'll do the same. When you get finished tomorrow come over and we will compare notes and make some plans."

The guilty feeling returned when she thought about the farm being taken from them. She forced the thoughts away as she put the kitchen back in order and stored leftovers in the refrigerator for him to eat later. She told herself not to feel bad for wanting to spend more time with him. She decided getting in trouble later was worth the risk. Anything could happen between now and the end of summer and who knows, they might not lose the farm.

Her father waved to her as she was getting in the jeep. She couldn't help but smile. It was so different from the way he treated her when she arrived. A feeling of excitement had her gunning the engine of the jeep as she left to go check the McCall's cotton fields. If it had rained there, she could get home quicker and start making plans. It had been a long time since she'd felt this hopeful that things just might work out after all.

Chapter Two

It seemed to Tyler McCall the pavement went on forever as he tried to stretch out his left leg attempting to get in a more comfortable position. He was having little success in easing the throbbing pain that was getting worse with each passing mile. Knowing now he should have taken the trip to visit his grandparents in stages didn't help. A frown of irritation crossed his brow as he gritted his teeth and tightened his grip on the steering wheel. He was determined that he would not give in to the white-hot pain that had become a persistent companion the last few months before reaching his grandparent's farm.

The breeze blowing through the opened window of his pickup felt good on his face. It was washed clean of dust by an early morning thundershower, evidence of the downpour still in potholes along the shoulders of the road. On each side of the highway were fields with rows and rows of young cotton plants that were greener than ever after the rain.

As the wind played lightly through his brown hair with its bronzed golden highlights his blue eyes were contemplating the passing scenery. Nothing changed much as one small town with its gas station, small grocery, a church or two, and sometimes a post office would give way to another community like the one before. A few houses lined the roadway, but each town would soon give way to pastureland, cotton fields, and once in while a pecan orchard.

He let out a sigh of relief when the southern delta city of Wilmot with its population sign of 361 came into view letting him know he was almost home. Tyler turned on his signal as he got close to the road that would take him to his grandparent's place. Turning onto the road he had to catch his breath in pain as he bumped over the railroad tracks. The road curved around a small lake, just a few more miles before he reached the final road that would put him on McCall land. A sign for the McCall Farm appeared and he turned onto it with another sigh. The graveled road was smooth trees crowded the road in places making it seem narrower than it actually was. He knew he was close when on the opposite side of the road the bayou with sunlight shimmering across its muddy surface appeared.

It was hard to believe the last time he visited his grandparents his life was altered so dramatically it would never be the same. A drunk teenage driver had crossed the center line and hit his car. Critically injured he had been told how lucky he was to have escaped with his life. A passenger in the other car had not been as lucky.

Tyler's hands gripped the steering wheel even more tightly because he was so tired of everyone telling him just how lucky he was. They did not have to have two surgeries and several months filled with pain and grueling physical therapy so they could at least walk with crutches. They did not have to deal with injuries that would forever keep them from fulfilling their career dreams. Yes, he had come home to recover, but he had also come home to seek his own revenge because someone was going to pay for what they had done to him.

Perhaps if he had been concentrating on his driving instead of being so absorbed in thoughts of the past and getting revenge, he would have seen the jeep coming around the curve sooner. He wrenched the steering wheel sharply to the right skidding in the loose gravel as he slammed on the brakes and the truck slid almost sideways. At the last moment when there should have been an impact, the jeep had gone into the ditch on the other side of the road. Thank goodness the road was no longer running beside the bayou.

Tyler found he was still gripping the steering wheel just sitting there trying to get his heart rate back to normal. He knew he had to get out and see about the other driver, but it was several seconds before he could make himself turn loose of the steering wheel. Several more seconds passed before the adrenaline finally kicked in and he could move at all. When he finally got out of the truck, he had trouble moving his legs. They were so stiff, and he had to reach across the seat for his crutches. By the time he was standing beside the truck, the driver of the jeep was getting out. He moved slowly forward and let out a sigh of relief when he realized the other driver wasn't hurt.

****

After her jeep had come to a stop in the deep ditch Jenny had been too shocked to move. Both hands were clenching the steering wheel so tightly that her knuckles were white. When she finally eased her grip on the steering wheel, she was glad of the seat belt holding her in the seat since the jeep was sitting almost on its side. She unbuckled the seatbelt and managed to climb onto the side of the jeep. The sunlight caught the highlights in her strawberry blond shoulder length hair matching the burning anger in her blue eyes. Some drivers thought they owned the road. Obviously, this was one of them. Jumping to the ground she rounded on the young man moving slowly toward her on crutches.

"Are you crazy? You could have gotten us both killed!" She was shouting, letting her temper get the best of her. She was five foot seven, but she had to tilt her head back to gaze into the handsome face of the man moving toward her. Her heart almost stopped then continued at a rapid pace as she recognized who she was shouting at, and she felt the color drain from her face. She wanted to take her words back and run in the opposite direction. *What if he recognized her?*

"No need to ask if you are all right." His voice was husky and low-pitched. Strong features were set in a serious expression, his face as white as hers felt.

"I wasn't hurt. What about you?" She asked in concern as she noticed the unconcealed pain showing in his eyes.

"No, I wasn't hurt," he spoke sharply. "This was my fault; I wasn't concentrating totally on my driving."

She was surprised that he admitted he was in the wrong. "I'm glad you are willing to acknowledge you were at fault," Jenny replied.

"Why?" Tyler asked, curious at her remark.

"I find most guys aren't willing to admit when they're at fault," she answered.

"I'll admit when I'm wrong, but this is essentially a private road, and I wasn't expecting to meet anyone."

"Then maybe you shouldn't be driving, Mr. McCall, because one should always drive expecting the unexpected." Jenny couldn't resist adding.

He gave her a hard glance, "It seems you are at an advantage here. You know who I am, but ..."

"Anyone who knows anything about sports knows who you are," she answered. "My name is Jenny. I scout cotton for your grandparents and will be driving this road quite often this summer. Even though it is essentially a private road you never know who you might run into out here."

"I'll keep that in mind in the future," he said. "Do you think since you know who I am, we might continue this chat somewhere else?"

Jenny noticed the paleness of his complexion and replied with concern, "I thought you said you weren't hurt?"

"It isn't this accident that's the problem. This leg is about to give out on me, and if I don't sit down soon, you're going to see me fall flat on my face."

"I'm sorry, I didn't think about your injury."

"Do you think you could drive me to my grandparent's house?" he rasped through gritted teeth. "Just let the tailgate down and I'll sit back here. I don't think I could get back in the cab right now."

"Of course," Jenny said, moving ahead of him toward his truck. She had the tailgate down where he could sit on it by the time he got to the truck. Once he sat down and moved further into the back, she helped him lift his injured leg up and straightened it out.

"What are you waiting for?" He barked with pain evident in his voice. "The keys are in the truck."

Jenny hurried around to the driver's seat. She had to adjust the seat before cranking the truck and driving slowly up the drive trying not to do any more damage to the man in the back. He probably wouldn't have let her anywhere near him or his truck if he had known her identity. She rounded another bend in the road and there in front of her was the two-story white framed farmhouse that was Thomas and Alma McCall's home. Tyler couldn't have found a better place to recuperate from his injuries, nor a better nurse to get him back on his feet.

The front door opened almost as soon as the truck pulled up. A tall, gray-haired woman stood in the opening, dressed in a loose-fitting cotton dress in calico-print with an apron tied around her waist. She hurried down the steps and out to the truck when she saw Tyler sitting in the back of the pickup.

"Tyler what on earth are you doing back there?" Alma reached the back of the truck in short order. "Jenny, what's happened?"

"Everything is fine Grandma, I am just having a little problem with this leg," he answered trying to get off the tailgate of the truck. The pain was evident in his white face and pain filled eyes. "Do you think you can help me get inside?"

"Of course, dear," Alma said helping him down and letting him stand a moment to get his balance.

It took both Alma and Jenny to get Tyler inside and to the front bedroom on the first floor that had been fixed up for him. He fell across the bed and put his head on the pillow. The moan he tried to silence told just how much pain he was in.

"When was the last time you had any pain medicine?" Alma asked, eyeing her grandson with concern.

"I couldn't take them and drive." He answered gruffly. "Besides I don't like taking them because of how they make me feel.

"Where are they now?" She asked in a no-nonsense voice.

He rolled over but kept his eyes closed. It was obvious that he hated anyone to see how much pain he was in. "They are in the glove compartment of the truck."

"Jenny, would you mind going and getting them?" Alma asked setting to work getting Tyler's shoes off.

"Sure, I will," Jenny agreed hurrying out to the truck for the pain medicine. When she opened the glove compartment the medicine was still in the paper sack that the pharmacist had put it in with the receipt attached. When she arrived back in the house Alma handed her a glass and told her to get some water while she looked at the prescription and took out the amount that Tyler could have. When Jenny got back with the water Alma handed her the pill.

"See if you can get that down him while I get an ice pack to put on his knee."

Tyler was still lying across the bed with his arm over his eyes. "Can you sit up and take your pain pill?"

He struggled to sit upright. Jenny handed him a pill and a glass of water. After swallowing the pill, he handed Jenny the glass and fell back on the bed. "You can go now."

"How long will you continue to have so much pain?" Jenny couldn't help but ask.

"Oh, the pain in the leg will get better in time, but the pain of losing my career will be with me for the rest of my life." Some of the bitterness he was feeling was evident in his voice. "I'm so sorry," Jenny said with tears in her voice. "I wish …" Tyler's eyes flew open. "Don't. I don't need you or anyone else feeling sorry for me." He said harshly.

Alma came back with the ice pack. "This should help ease the pain some as well."

"I need to go," Jenny said as she backed toward the door.

"Tyler told me about your jeep. I was able to reach Thomas on his cell and he said to tell you he will be here shortly. He will see if he can help your jeep out of the ditch."

"Thanks, I'll wait for him out front." Jenny said before hurrying from the room. She needed to get away from Tyler McCall. It hurt to see him in so much pain and hear him talk so cynically about his loss. What a way to finally meet someone you had admired from afar for so long. But worst to almost run into him for a second time. What would he say when he found out who she really was? He was going to be angry there was no doubt about that, only God knew what he had come home to do.

She felt a desire to ask God to make all of this right, but just as quickly she felt it would do little good. No matter how much she wanted the past to change there was no way of going back and changing what could not be changed. Dead was dead unless you were Jesus. Why would God want to help someone who lied and who many thought of as a murderer anyway?

Chapter Three

When Thomas pulled up to get Jenny, she quickly wiped tears away and put a smile on her face. Both Alma and he had been good to her since the accident and had hired her to scout their cotton so she would have a summer job. It took only a few minutes to go back to where Tyler had run her off the road into the ditch. When they arrived at the jeep two of the other farm workers were already there and had the jeep back up on the road.

"Looks like we are too late to help." Thomas said with a smile as he pulled up behind the jeep.

Climbing out of the 4-wheel drive pickup, Jenny quickly looked at the jeep to see if there was any damage. There was nothing to indicate there was anything wrong so hopefully, she wouldn't have to get anything fixed. The jeep was her only mode of transportation so she really hoped there would be no further problems.

"Thanks for getting it out." She told the two men.

"I don't think there is any damage underneath. Everything sounded fine and there weren't any problems when we used the 4-wheel drive to help get it out of the ditch."

Jenny got in the vehicle and cranked it up. It sounded fine and when she put it in gear it moved forward like it always did. She gave the men a wave and drove off. The distance into Wilmot was covered in a matter of minutes. She drove through the small town and around the lake to a small wood-framed house just on the outskirts. A large red lab came around the corner of the house barking while his tail wagged a greeting. Tall oaks shaded the house, and she was glad to be out of the sun where it felt a good ten degrees cooler.

"Down, Red!" she laughed at the dog's friendly greeting. He immediately obeyed her command. "Good Boy," Jenny said patting his head a moment before entering the house through the back door. The small kitchen was connected to a dining area that opened into a large living room. Red followed her into the house and went to lie down on his dog bed near the back door. He rested his face on his paws and looked up at her like he was saying thank you for letting me into the cool house.

"Jenny?" Is that you?" A female voice called from the far corner of the living room where, a small gray-haired woman sat behind a quilting frame quilting.

"It's me." Jenny answered closing the door behind her. The house was cool by a window air-conditioner but the temperature inside was just pleasant because the older woman couldn't stand for the temperature to be too cool.

"Where in the world have you been child?" Ruth asked. "You're usually home on rainy days by now."

"I got stuck out on the McCall road."

"Stuck? How'd you manage that?"

"Well actually, Tyler McCall ran me off the road." Jenny said. Her voice held none of the emotions she was feeling.

Jenny looked over at the tiny gray-haired figure sitting bent over the quilt. Ruth Phillips was a cantankerous old woman, but she had taken Jenny in and given her a place to stay at a time when no one else would. She would always be grateful to her for that, and she had been allowed to see a side of Ruth that few people ever saw that was giving and loving. She really cared about those close to her. She reminded Jenny of another Ruth, the one in the *Bible* who loved Naomi, her mother-in-law, so much she followed her back to her home country after Naomi's husband and two sons had died.

Jenny's grandmother often read the story of Ruth to her and they had memorized the verse in the *Bible* from Ruth 1:16, where Ruth said to Naomi, "Intreat me not to leave thee, or to return from following after thee; for whither thou goest, I will go; and where thou lodgest, I will lodge; thy people shall be my people, and thy God my God." Her grandmother had told her several times how those words had been a part of her wedding vows. Her grandparents had been so happy together and God had certainly been the center of their marriage. She just knew if one day she found someone to love as much as her grandmother loved her grandfather that she too would want those words included in her own wedding vows.

Ruth gave her a hard look. "Why on earth did he do a fool thing like that for?"

"I really think he was in so much pain from his injured leg his driving wasn't as it should be," Jenny replied as she walked over to the quilt and touched the tiny stitches. She admired Ruth's handwork and the effort she put into her quilt.

"Then he shouldn't be driving." Ruth said.

"He's come for the trial probably." Jenny sighed.

"Maybe he just wants to spend some time with his grandparents while getting back on his feet," Ruth suggested. "The trial is not until the first of August."

"He's pretty bitter about his leg." Grimness pulled at her mouth and with a frustrated movement she turned to walk over by a window that looked out on the street in front of the house.

"He's only human," Ruth commented mildly as gentle brown eyes looked across the quilt at the young girl, she had taken in.

"Why do you think they let me scout their cotton?" Jenny asked. "It's not like they couldn't have found someone else to do it."

"I don't know but it might be because you are a fine person, Jenny Reynolds. They were good friends with your grandparents and that could have something to do with it as well. I took it, Tyler didn't know your identity."Not yet, I only said my name was Jenny," she replied a sad wistful look on her face. "He will find out soon enough and then he will hate me like everyone else."

"I'm so sorry, honey," Ruth said. "I know it's hard, and I don't mean to add to your troubles, but your court-appointed attorney called to talk today. He wants to talk to you about making a deal for a reduced sentence and keeping everything out of court. If you ask me the fellow is not much of a public defender." Ruth's feeling toward the lawyer was very evident in her voice."What's the catch?" Jenny knew there had to be one. It would be great to have all this behind her, but nothing would bc that easy, especially when dealing with Ted Smith, the father of her best friend.

"You go directly to a correction facility and the Smiths get your grandparent's farm and money your grandparents left you in their will."

"That would be Anita's dad getting the courts to do his will," Jenny said. "How long would I be in the correction facility?"

"Till you are eighteen." Ruth replied, making a face. "You don't belong in one of those places."

"One year," Jenny cried.

"Go to court, Jenny. At least you stand a chance of not having to go to that place."

"I'm scared." Jenny admitted to Ruth. "I sometimes think I am in a bad dream, and I will never wake up. Just today, Dad finally let me in, but he turned his back and walked away without saying a word. He didn't say hi or anything other than for me to go away before opening the door. Then when he came back in from the barn, he acted completely different."

"I wish I could fix things for you, honey," Ruth said. "Maybe he just needed to wake up before he was ready to talk."

"I made him lunch and he came in and ate. We talked a little."

"At least he ate with you," Ruth commented continuing to make tiny stitches as she moved her needle up and down through the material of the quilt.

"At times he seems okay and in the next instance he's different again," Jenny admitted. "I don't know what to think anymore. I wish I could talk to his doctors, but I wouldn't even know where to start and I don't know if they would even talk to me."

"I don't know what to tell you," Ruth said. "What are you going to do about the attorney?"

"I'm going to go to court, mainly because I don't know where my father will stay if we lose the farm right now. I'm not even sure how he will deal with all of this when he learns the truth," Jenny said walking back into the room.

"Honey, you're going to have to tell him."

"I know," Jenny told her. "Today when I was there, I checked the mail and there was a large check in the mailbox that had been there for days. Dad says we are going to try and get the roof fixed and maybe fix the old house up some too. I wanted to tell him then."

"You have to tell him about the Smith's threat to take the farm!"

"I just couldn't bring myself to destroy the good mood he was in after the start of our morning. He seemed different somehow when he came back in."

"Who knows, maybe helping fix the place up will give your father something to focus on instead of on his injuries." Ruth said. "Don't worry yourself so. You know what the good book says. Your heavenly Father knows what you require, and he will supply. You'll see, you mark my words, he will supply."

"He certainly supplied you when I needed you," Jenny said walking over to give her a hug. "Now all I need is to have a little faith that he will take care of the rest."

"That's the attitude. Expect something good to come of all of this and it will."

Jenny wanted to have Ruth's faith, but she was still afraid of what the future held in store for her. Glancing at the clock on the wall she noticed it was time to let the County Extension Office know she was unable to scout any of the cotton fields that morning because of the rain. "Do you need me to run any errands before I email my report?"

"Not today," Ruth replied. "There are some leftovers in the refrigerator if you're hungry."

"I'm okay," Jenny answered as she headed toward her room. "I think I'll get this email out of the way first."

Entering her room, Jenny's eyes immediately fell on the full-length poster of Tyler McCall as he was going up for a jump shot. The strength was not only in the pose of his body but in the determined look on his young face. He was in his Razorback basketball uniform and the poster shot had been on the cover of *Sports Illustrated* magazine when the Razorback's won the National Championship his freshmen year at the University of Arkansas. At nineteen he was a force with lots of promise. Now at twenty, his dreams had been dashed by one reckless night of bad decisions. No matter how much regret was involved there were just some things that even prayers couldn't change.

Moving over to a dresser in one corner of the room she picked up a picture frame. The faces of two girls and a tall boy with their arms linked around each other with big smiles beamed back. Mark and Anita Smith were twins and her best friends until the accident. The three had been together more than they were apart. They had no cares or worries, but all of that had been changed in a matter of seconds. The memory was so fresh it might have been yesterday instead of seven months earlier. Every time she reviewed the chain of events that took place that night, she still didn't know of any way she could have prevented what happened. Mark was dead and Anita hadn't talked to her since. Anita's father and her brother, Willie, had called her a murderer and shouted she would pay for the life she had taken.

Ted Smith would have done Ruth and her harm the day they went to court if it had not been for Bob Warren, the County Sheriff. He had stood between Jenny and Mark's father. He had also arranged for Ruth to ask the court to allow her to live with her until a court date that summer. She would forever be grateful to them both for what they did for her that day. Ted had called Ruth a crazy old woman and declared Jenny deserved to go to jail for what she had done.

The picture faded as her eyes misted over, teardrops landing on the glass. She felt a strong need to talk to Anita, but nothing was going to bring Mark back or heal Tyler's injured leg so he could play basketball again. The reality was it was too late. There was no going back, no way to change what happened that night. She finally placed the picture back on the dresser and moved over to the computer and turned it on. Keep busy, that was what she must do, keep so busy that she didn't have time to think about what might have been. *Lord no matter how many prayers I pray, there is no changing the past. Mark is dead, and I am still here trying to deal with the life I now have. Please be with Anita, I know she is in such pain. Help her to heal and be able to deal with her brother's death.*

Chapter Four

"No!" Tyler put his arm up to ward off the car coming straight at him. He couldn't get out of the way. He could feel the pain in his leg, and he couldn't move it.

"Tyler are you okay?" his grandmother's voice awoke him.

He was all tangled up in the covers and his leg was in an uncomfortable position. Letting out a sigh he was relieved it was only having another one of his nightmares. Sweat beaded his forehead, and he had an awful taste in his mouth that said he had taken pain medicine again. He hated taking it and he hated the way he felt when he woke up afterward.

"Here, let's get some of this cover straighten out and see if we can get your leg in a more comfortable position." Alma quickly untangled the covers and placed a pillow under his leg. "Now, is that better?"

"Much, thank you." Tyler sighed again. "What I would really like is a shower."

"Give yourself a little time and make sure the pain medicine has worn off enough. We don't want another injury."

"How long have I been out?" Tyler questioned.

"About six hours, it is almost seven." his grandmother informed him with a smile.

Tyler looked surprised. "I didn't realize I had been out that long."

"You needed the rest, and the medicine helped."

"I don't like taking it," he responded. "I feel so out of it once I wake up."

"Right now, your body is trying to recover its strength, and you need to be able to rest."

"That's what my doctor said, but I knew if I took the pills, I wouldn't be able to drive here."

"Well, you are here now, and our goal is to get you back on your feet and back to getting around without those crutches."

"Where's Gramps?"

"He's on the front porch enjoying the sunset."

Tyler slowly sets up on the side of the bed, using his hands to get his leg to the floor. He didn't try to stand up yet, he was sure he would fall on his face, and he didn't want to cause his grandmother any more worry than he already had.

"Sorry about the way I arrived, I didn't mean to scare you," Tyler said.

"I'm just glad you're here, so we can get you back on your feet and feeling fit again."

"Just don't expect it to happen overnight," Tyler stated knowing all too well how long each step seemed to take to get him completely well. He was hopeful that this last surgical treatment was just that, his last surgery on his knee. He knew he still had a long way to go.

"It'll take a little time, but you'll see by the time summer is over you'll be a different man."

"I hope so Gran, I sure hope so."

"Just sit on the side of the bed for a few minutes and let yourself get adjusted to sitting up and get your balance back while I turn on the shower for you. I unpacked your clothes while you slept. What do you want to wear?"

"Shorts and a t-shirt will be fine."

"I'll put them in the bathroom and get you some towels."

Tyler could hear the water being turned on. Carefully, he stood up and used his crutches to move slowly toward the bathroom. At first, the room whirled but he quickly gained his balance.

"Everything you need should be right here. Get your shower and I'll fix you a ham and cheese omelet. Come on out on the porch when you are ready."

Tyler soon felt better just standing under the warm shower and would have spent more time there if his stomach wasn't grumbling. Once out of the shower it took him a little time to get dried off and dressed. When he reached the door to go out on the porch his grandmother already had a chair ready and a footstool and pillow for his leg. She was there helping him into the chair and positioning his leg so he was as comfortable as she could make him.

"Now Gran, you aren't to wait on me hand and foot," Tyler said with regret that he needed her help now.

"Just today, Tyler," she laughed. "Tomorrow you will feel better, and I'll let you do for yourself."

"Promise."

"I see you know your grandmother," Thomas McCall laughed as he looked over at his grandson.

"Oh Thomas, you know I love waiting on him," she said liking her husband's teasing by the twinkle in her eyes as they met Tyler's. "I promise I will let you do as much as you feel like as soon as you feel like doing it. Now, you had better take care of this omelet while it is still warm."

Tyler smiled at his grandmother as she moved a TV tray across his lap. "This smells wonderful." His mouth was watering just thinking about how good he knew it would taste.

Thomas McCall laughed at his grandson again. "If you're ever lucky enough to find yourself a good cook like your grandmother, you had better marry her, my boy."

"Any chance you have some of your famous cinnamon rolls?" Tyler asked.

"How did you guess?" Alma laughed, the expression on her face expressing she was pleased by his question.

"I thought I smelled them," Tyler answered. "My mouth is watering for one."

"Eat your omelet first," she replied. "Then I'll see if I can find you a couple with some milk before bedtime. I think your granddad would like to play you in a game of chess when you feel up to it."

"Good to have you here for a while Tyler," His grandfather said after his grandmother stopped fussing and went inside.

"You don't know how good it is to be here." Tyler replied. "Just wish I was well so we could do all the fun stuff we usually do when I visit."

"I think I can understand." His grandfather commented. "Especially, since I have had to slow down a little this past year."

"Was the jeep much trouble to get out of the ditch this afternoon?" Tyler asked.

"No problem. By the time Jenny and I got back to it Ed and Frank had it out."

"She said she scouts your cotton." Tyler added. "She looks a little young to be scouting."

"That's right. She scouts for us and does a fine job too." Thomas said. "I think she is seventeen. I know she will be a senior this coming school year."

"I'd like to thank her for her help."

"I'm sure you'll get a chance in the next few days," his grandfather said. "She is on the farm most days."

Chapter Five

By early afternoon the following day, Jenny had finished her scouting and paperwork in record time. On arriving at the homeplace she was bewildered by the number of trucks parked in the driveway. As she scanned the scene in front of her, she was surprised to see a half-dozen men up on the roof of the house. She saw her father near the porch talking to another man on the ground. When she was closer, she was able to tell it was Bob Warren the county sheriff, one of her father's old buddies. He wasn't in uniform today so he must be there as a friend. On closer inspection, she noticed that several of the men on the roof were also in law enforcement.

"Bet you weren't expecting the roof to be almost finished when you arrived, did you?" her father said as she walked up to him.

"You did surprise me," Jenny replied as she smiled at both men.

"Hey Jenny," Bob Warren said. "Good to see you here today."

"Hello Mr. Warren," she answered. "I can't believe this."

"I told your dad a while back we would help do this job. Glad he decided to let us."

"There are some things on the kitchen table you might want to look at, Jenny," her father indicated she could go on in. "I'll be there in just a moment."

"I brought my list too," she said holding up a notebook.

She went into the house. When she arrived in the kitchen, she found several different floor samples and several folders with different paint colors. After looking at them and some of the brochures her father had picked up, she decided she liked the wood floor the best. Walking into the hallway where the floor covering needing replacing as well, she decided the wood floor would look good throughout the bottom floor. She liked the lighter shade, but she would check with her father on which he liked.

Sitting down at the kitchen table she read the prices for each type of flooring and what it would cost to install. Looking in the utility room for a measuring tape she measured the kitchen and down the hallway. The den was in good shape so she didn't know if her dad would want to do anything about the floor in there, so she didn't measure it. She was finishing up the measuring in the living room when the hammering from outside stopped. Wondering if they were taking a break, she looked out the front windows and noticed that several men were getting in their trucks and leaving.

She went back to the kitchen and worked on finding out how many square feet of flooring they would need to do the kitchen, hallway, and living room. Then she took the two she liked best and figured the cost of each. There was a small difference so whichever her father liked they could go with. As she looked at the brochures, she found two colors of paint in creams and tans that she really thought would go well in the living room. The sofa and chairs in the picture were furnishings she thought she would like to check out. It had been a long time since there had been any new living room furniture bought for the house and she would love to purchase one of those new recliners for her dad for Father's Day.

After making herself a glass of iced tea she had just sat back down at the kitchen table when her father came in.

"Well, what do you think?" He said going over to the refrigerator and taking out a Pepsi and popping the top before taking a big swig. Lowering the drink, he looked across the table at Jenny.

"I'm very impressed. When you say you are going to do something you get right on it." She laughed at the pleased look on his face.

"The only hold up on the roof has been the money to buy the shingles and other roofing materials. Bob has been on me every time he's been by to get the work done. When I saw him at the bank yesterday and asked him if he could recommend anyone for the roofing job, he said he was available to do the job today. I didn't know he was going to bring so many people. While they tore the old shingles off and fixed the boards that needed fixing, Bob went with me to get the new shingles and other materials. With their help, we now have a new roof."

"Hooray! No more buckets and pans, and I, for one, am glad about that." Jenny admitted as she passed her dad the estimate for the floor covering. "I wanted your opinion of the wood flooring. Do you like the dark or light wood?"

"The prices are about the same, so you tell me which you like best?" Dave said.

"Now Dad," she began.

He cut off her objection by declaring, "Seriously, your grandmother and you liked a lot of the same things. Which do you think she would like the best?"

"At first, I thought I would like the lighter wood the most, but after looking at these booklets, I think the darker wood might be something grandma would have loved."

"And you," he countered.

"Yes, I love it." She reached for the brochures and showed her father the picture of the dark flooring with the two-tone tan paint colors. "Look at this, what do you think about something like this. We could use it in the living room, hallway, and blend it in with some new wallpaper for the kitchen. The wood on the cabinets would also work well with the colors and the dark flooring."

"You know, I think you are right." he said as he looked at the picture. "The lighter colors on the walls will also make the rooms seem bigger, or at least that is what I have always heard."

"Rooms are big now but look at the big pieces of furniture in this picture. I think a living room suit like this one would look so good in the living room." Jenny showed her father what she was talking about.

"We'll work on the flooring and painting first. But I'll admit I've been thinking about getting some new furniture for the living room. Is there anything in there you would want to keep?"

"Are you kidding? I think some of that stuff must have come over in the Mayflower." Jenny laughed and for the first time since he had been back, her father laughed too. It was a good sound and Jenny hoped it would be the first of many to come.

"I'm going to get some prices on new insulated windows with the wood look and I was thinking about knocking out some walls on the back of the house and adding a sunroom."

"Do you remember how Grandma used to talk about doing that?" Jenny asked.

"Yeah, what do you think?"

"I like the idea, and I know Grandma would if she were here."

"Now, that we have that settled," he stated. "I have something I need to talk to you about."

"Sure dad," Jenny said sat back in her chair and gave her father her full attention. She already knew it was about Mark and the accident.

"The reason I saw Bob yesterday at the bank was because I had a little problem with Ted Smith."

"What kind of problem?" Jenny asked, apprehensive of the answer. She already knew what her father was going to say, or at least a pretty good idea.

"I'm at the teller window depositing my checks when he comes out of the office with the bank manager. He comes running up behind me shouting something about my daughter was going to pay for killing his son," her father said. "I'm afraid my reaction with him shouting and rushing me was to turn and take him down to the floor with his face planted on the floor and his arms pinned behind his back. I can't say I was proud of what I did, it was an automatic reaction. It took me back to a place I didn't want to go."

"Oh Dad," Jenny declared surprised by her father's confession. "You didn't get arrested?"

"No, but we both had to go to city hall and fill out some paperwork. Bob just happened to be here and came to the bank when the call went out. He talked to both of us and Ted was not doing as much yelling by the time he got done with him." Dave Reynolds said. "I was a little embarrassed by my reaction. And that's one of the reasons I pretty much stay to myself and away from other people. Including you Jenny, I don't want to hurt you."

"I'm not afraid of you hurting me, Dad."

"I just sometimes have these really bad headaches," Dave replied. "Until they're better its best you stay where you are."

"So, you know about what happened to Mark?"

"I'm not going to ask you why you didn't tell me." He said but it was plain to see by the look on his face that he was disappointed that she had not shared this with him. "I know I should have told you, and I had a chance yesterday. Dad, I wanted more time with you. I didn't want to ruin it by having to tell you Ted Smith is going to try and take the farm away from us."

"Do you want to tell me about the accident?"

"There's not much to tell, it was an accident. Mark died and Tyler McCall was injured and will never play basketball again. I haven't talked to Anita since we were in the emergency room and her father came in screaming at us for killing his son," Jenny said. "Anita kept saying it was her, it was her. They had to take her father out still screaming at me. What else can I say? It was the worst day of my life and nothing I say or do will ever change anything that happened that night."

"You don't usually drink, so how come you were drinking that night?"

"I don't drink alcohol, Dad. I'm not sure, but I now think the punch was spiked at the school dance. I promise I didn't know, and I didn't even drink that much, but I guess it was enough to show up in the blood test they did on me that night."

"Bob said there were several students who witnessed you driving Mark's car when you left the dance," Dave said. "Why wasn't Mark driving?"

"Mark was being really silly at the time and was stumbling around a lot. I'm pretty sure he had drunk a lot of the punch," Jenny replied. "I don't remember him having the smell of any kind of alcohol on him though."

"What else do you remember?"

"Dad, I really don't want to talk about it," Jenny began to cry softly, and her father looked like he didn't know what to do to help his daughter. She wasn't a little girl anymore and he realized she had grown into a young woman without him even noticing. Where had the time gone?

"How did you come to be in Ruth's care?" he asked.

"She came to court and stood up for me at the hearing. I think Bob Warren pulled some strings that may have had something to do with it. Ted Smith shouted at her that day and would have harmed us both if he could have. You know what she might be a small woman but in her quiet way, she silenced him. We walked out of the courthouse with her as my appointed guardian until the trial in August."

"Do you have an attorney who is working for you?"

"I have a court appointed attorney, but I think he's working with Ted Smith's attorney. Ruth said he wants me to sign a deal they have worked on, so I'll go to a correction center for a year. Of course, the Smith's get the farm and the money that was left for me in a trust by grandpa and grandma's will."

He looked angry at the last information. "I think I am going to fire your appointed attorney and hire someone I know who will fight for you. Saying that I wish I could have been here for you through all of this is a little late."

"I'm really sorry, Dad," Jenny said with tears still in her voice. "I won't say no to the new attorney because I really don't want to go to a correction facility. The attorney the court appointed never talks to me. It was always to Ruth. I don't think he is doing much for me anyway."

"That will be enough for now," he added. "We'll visit this again. What would you say we go fishing down at the pond?"

"Do you think grandpa's worms are still there?" Jenny questioned.

"I've already checked it out," he replied letting a small smile show.

"Then what are we waiting for?" She dried her tears and headed for the kitchen door. When she reached the porch, her father had fishing poles and the worms already waiting. She turned back toward him and smiled. It felt good knowing her father knew and they would face her problems together. *Thank You, Lord, I really need my dad on my side. I appreciate any help I can get.*

Chapter Six

It had been over a week since Jenny had driven Tyler up to his grandparent's house. As she turned up the driveway, she found him out walking. Pulling the jeep up beside him as he walked up the drive to the farmhouse she said, "You look a lot better today."

"I feel better, but I'm ready to lose these," he said as he held one of the crutches up.

"What are you doing today?" Jenny asked.

"Why?"

"I'm checking boll weevil traps. Would you like to ride along and help?"

"Okay, but I need to stop and let Gran know where I'll be," Tyler replied.

"Get in and I'll run you up to the house."

Tyler put the crutches in the back and slowly got into the jeep. They drove up to the house where Jenny stopped in the shade to wait for him. He got out and reached for the crutches in the back before going into the house. The smile he flashed at Jenny had her catching her breath while her heartbeat faster.

"Don't you dare leave without me," he shouted when he had taken a couple of steps. "I won't be long."

When Tyler came back out his grandmother followed behind carrying a picnic basket in one hand and a small cooler in the other.

"Hi Jenny. I thought you might find a spot for lunch before bringing this guy back. I'm afraid he needs company other than us old folks." She handed Jenny the basket with a big smile on her face.

"I know just the place." Jenny laughed. "I hope you put some of your famous cinnamon rolls in here."

"Am I going to have to fight you for Gran's cinnamon rolls?" Tyler asked.

"Oh, I might let you have at least one."

"Have fun you two," Alma said looking pleased with herself. "And don't hurry back."

"If you'll call Miss Ruth for me, I'll see about keeping him out for most of the day," Jenny replied as she backed the jeep up and pulled out heading for the first of the boll weevil traps. Driving carefully, she tried to miss the large potholes in the road so she wouldn't bounce Tyler around too much. On reaching the first trap she pulled as close as possible to the green trap on Tyler's side so he could reach it without getting out of the vehicle.

"Have you ever checked traps before?" she asked as he reached out for the first one.

"Can't say that I have," he replied handing it to her.

She took the trap and opened it up. Inside were two little boll weevils, true enemies to a cotton crop.

"You would think they're too small to cause such a fuss, but too many of these and a cotton crop will be in trouble." Removing the little critters, she placed a small tab of bait back inside before handing it to Tyler to put it back on the pole while she recorded the information on her recording sheet.

"What do you do with the information you gather?" Tyler asked.

"I send it to the County Extension Agency who takes it and records it. They use the information to help determine if the cotton needs to be sprayed. The data we gather includes the number of weevils in the traps or the number and kinds of insects and worms found in the field. It can save farmers a lot of money and is one of the reasons scouts need to do their jobs correctly."

"Your job sounds like an important one."

"It is. Like I said it helps determine if the fields need to be sprayed or treated for insects. It helps the farmer, and as you can see, I have plenty of traps to check."

The morning passed quickly. Having Tyler there to help with the traps cut down on the time it normally took for her to check them when she was alone.

"Do you not have someone to scout with?" Tyler said as they left their last field. "I would think it would be a little dangerous being out and about all by yourself."

"Most of the fields are in good locations, and if I need help, I have my CB radio and my cell phone."

"You still use a CB radio?" He sounded surprised.

"What can I say, it came with the jeep." She laughed.

"It's not on now."

"I only use it if I need to, but today I have you," She didn't bother to tell him there would be no one who would care to talk to her anyway. Sometimes she had it on just to hear another human voice besides her own.

She took a gravel road that led away from the cotton field. A short time later she turned down a small lane that led to a place where all that was left of the house was the charred remains of a chimney outlined the landscape. Jenny drove past the house and followed the lane to the back of the property where a large pond was shaded on two sides by large cypress trees. Parking near one of the trees she got out and took a quilt and the picnic basket toward a clearing near the bank of the pond. Placing the quilt in the shade she put the basket on it and turned to go back for the cooler. Tyler had managed to hook the cooler over his arm and was moving slowly toward her.

Laughing she waited till he reached her before taking it from him. She placed it beside the picnic basket and sat down and spread out their meal. There were several sandwiches, chips, fruit, and the famous cinnamon rolls. There were also paper plates and forks, although Jenny doubted, they were needed until she noticed the container of potato salad.

Tyler took his time sitting down. He was exercising his legs after spending the last three hours riding around checking the traps. It was obvious it had become stiff. Once he was seated on the quilt, he stretched his legs out and propped his body up on one elbow. He looked comfortable.

"You look like you've done this before," Jenny said into the silence.

"Actually, not too many times. This is about the only way I can get comfortable with this leg."

Jenny passed him a paper plate and let him choose what he wanted to eat. She loaded her own plate with a little of everything, leaving the cinnamon rolls and fruit until later. Tossing him a drink she popped the top of her Coke and took a long cool swallow. Although it was early June the temperature was in the low nineties and the drink was very refreshing. They ate in silence for several minutes.

"Aren't we trespassing?" Tyler asked.

"The lady I live with knows the owners. I have permission to come here to swim or fish whenever I feel like it or have time." Jenny replied.

"Will they rebuild?"

"Some of the family might, but the owners in a nursing home now. Mrs. McDonald has Alzheimer's and needs constant care. Mr. McDonald is lost without her. It's really sad. I know they've had a good life, but to not be remembered by those you love must be very painful."

"I'm sure you're right," Tyler said. "Now pass me one of those cinnamon rolls."Jenny did as he asked. She enjoyed her cinnamon roll before licking icing off her fingers. As she looked up, she noticed Tyler staring at her with a smile on his face. For something to do, she begins to put the picnic things back in the basket which took little time.

"Come here," Tyler requested as he finished up his cinnamon roll. She wasn't sure what he wanted.

"What?" She laughed at the expression on his face.

"Come here and sit down right here for a minute," he said grinning at her.

She moved over to where he pointed. When she was seated, he eased his head onto her lap.

"Now," he sighed. "That's much more like it." He closed his eyes with a happy smile on his face. A few minutes later he was sound asleep. Jenny sat very still and let him sleep. She felt a strong desire to brush his hair back on his forehead but was afraid to move in case she woke him up. He was so handsome, and she knew this was probably the only opportunity she would have to be this close to him.

She was enjoying a chance to be this close to someone she had had a crush on for a couple of years. What he would think of that if he knew, she didn't even want to consider. Once he learned who she was he wouldn't want to have anything to do with her. She felt his eyes on her.

"What are you thinking?" He asked.

"Why?"

"You had such a sad look in your eyes, almost as if you were in pain."

"I guess I was thinking about how different my life is than what I thought it would be," she answered.

"Yeah, I can relate to that. Last year I thought I would be this great basketball star, and I would never have considered something like my accident happening. Now, I'm going to have to rethink what I want to do with the rest of my life."

"I'm sorry."

"It's not your fault that some kid got drunk and wrecked my life," he said bitterly. He sits up. "I sometimes just want to get my hands on that person. That's why I'm here, to see she suffers for what she did."

"You sound as if you hate that person."

"I hate what she did to me," Tyler said angrily. "I know we are supposed to forgive people when they hurt us, but right now I just want to make her hurt like I do. She is going to pay. After all, she killed one of the riders in the car."

Jenny got quickly to her feet and started picking up their stuff to put back in the jeep. She had to keep her hands busy, they were shaking so much that she knew Tyler would notice. With her back to him, she couldn't resist asking, "What makes you so sure that she hasn't suffered?"

"I guess you know her, and she is a friend of yours."

"I know she lost two friends that night. Don't you think she's suffering knowing she contributed to her friend's death?"

"Yeah, I guess that might be true."

"Just don't think you're the only one who has lost here." Jenny took the things to the jeep and started storing them for the ride home. The day had started out looking up, but it only took the sharp reminder to bring her back to the reality of what she still had to face. "Perhaps it's time you stop feeling sorry for yourself and be thankful that you're still around to enjoy life." Once the words were out there was no way to take them back.

"I'm not feeling sorry for myself," he declared in a tone that indicated differently. The stormy look on his face almost stopped her from continuing.

"No, then why are you whining about something you can't change?" she asked.

"I'm not!"

"Yes, you are!"

"What would you know about failed dreams?"

"Maybe more than you'll ever know," Jenny replied going over to get in the jeep.

Jenny was very quiet on the drive back. She really didn't know what to say to Tyler. One thing she did know, she wasn't ready to have him as an enemy. Was it so wrong to want to spend a little more time with him? She knew once he knew the truth of who she was he was going to hate her. There was an uncomfortable silence as they traveled back the way they came.

They were pulling into the McCall's driveway when she said, "Sorry if I spoke out of turn, but I do know without purpose your life isn't likely to go anywhere."

"Right now, I do have a purpose," Tyler declared. "I came to see Jennifer Reynolds pays for what she did to me. After that, I'll decide what I'm going to do for the rest of my life. Thanks for letting me go today." Jenny paled as he finished. She knew he meant her, but he didn't know that. She had to get out and put the picnic basket and the cooler on the front steps.

"I have to get back" she said. "I still have to get my report to the County Extension Office."

"I'm going to see some friends I meet in college next Tuesday. Would you like to go?" Tyler asked. "It will be around two in the afternoon, so you should be finished with scouting."

Even knowing she was being unfair to Tyler and that their friendship would soon end, she couldn't refuse the invitation. "Sure, I would like to go," she said. A smile appeared on her face as she drove away when she heard Tyler whistling as he made his way inside. Even after the words she had said to him he still wanted to go somewhere with her.

Chapter Seven

"Hey, I wasn't expecting to see you here," Jenny said as she opened the door of the jeep and found Christy Rivers, a classmate, sitting on the porch with Red. Christy was one of the few friends that had stayed in touch with her after the accident. She was what Jenny felt a true friend should be, standing beside a friend no matter what.

"My grandmother is picking up a quilt that Miss Ruth made for her," Christy replied as she gave Jenny a quick hug. "I came with her so I could see if you would be interested in performing with some of us on the 4th of July. We've been asked to be part of the program by singing some patriotic songs just before the firework show. Also, to see if you have any suggestions for what we might sing."

"I don't think that would be a good idea. I would hate to get tomatoes, or something thrown at you because of me being in the group," Jenny answered with regret in her voice.

"I'm sorry Jenny." Christy said. "I know all of this is hard on you. We would still love for you to be part of the program."

"I understand why people treat me so different now," Jenny replied. "I know most of it's because so many people loved and cared about Mark. They hate that he's gone. But I miss him too, I would do anything to have him back."

"I'm sorry you are having to deal with all of this. I know Mr. Smith has really been stirring things up too." Christy added. "How things will ever get back to normal with all his comments in both the paper and out in the community is beyond comprehension. His son, Willie, isn't any better, some of the comments he has made worries me. You need to watch your back and be careful when you go out."

Jenny knew from the concern on her friend's face these were not idol comments.

"I'm scouting the McCall's fields and they're in pretty safe areas. I don't think Mr. Smith or Willie could afford to do anything that might damage their chances in court to get my grandparent's farm. Mr. Smith would be all over Willie if he thought he might get in the way of that happening," Jenny said. "I've recently been spending some time with my dad who is finally home. We're working on my grandparent's place, fixing it up some. "I'm glad your dad is doing better."

"Me too," Jenny replied.

Christy held up her phone and said, "I have a song I want you to hear. I think it might help when you're down. It is a new song by Matthew West called "*The God Who Stays*" and I just love the lyrics."

Jenny watches the screen with her friend and the words touched her, helping her realize she did have a friend when all the others turned away because she still had God. She found herself humming the tune and singing the chorus. "You're the God who stays,,, You're the God who stays… You're the one who runs in my direction… when the whole world walks away… You're the God who stands… with wide open arms… You tell me nothing I have ever done… can separate my heart… from the God who stays…"

With tears streaming down her face, she smiles at Christy, but words wouldn't come. She was thankful Christy was a friend who stayed and had reminded her that she was not alone. When the song was over Jenny was so glad that Christy had shared the song with her. She knew she would be playing it when she felt alone in the future.

"Thanks, Christy. That song filled a void. It's like God knew I needed to hear it, and He sent you today with a message I needed reminded of."

"I'm glad if it helps," Christy replied.

"Talking about songs for the program, I did hear a song recently that might be a good one to sing. I found it by accident when listening to some patriotic songs. I'm sure you are going to sing *God Bless America*?"

"It's on our list."

"Well, this song is called *America Bless God*," Jenny said. "I believe it was written and sang by Abigail Miller and has a good message. You really need to be sure to check it out. Just type in lyrics for America Bless God by Abigail Miller in the computer."

"I will when I get home. Do you ever hear anything from Anita?" Christy asked softly like she was unsure if she should even be asking.

"No, I wish I could talk to her, but Mr. Smith said I can't."

"I know that has to be hard on you," Christy said. "I'm sorry, Jenny, you have to go through all of this alone."

"Miss Ruth has been a big help," Jenny said with tears in her eyes as she looked at Christy. "It's been a long time since anyone said anything about how Anita is doing. I think not knowing is the hardest part in all of this."

"Jenny, I know you believe in God." Christy stated. "That's one of the reasons I thought the song I let you hear could be a help."

"You know I do, but I'm sure He isn't too happy with me right now. Sometimes I talk to Him, but I can't seem to get past all of this, it's like I am frozen or something."

"Did you know since you are His, He already knows? The *Bible* says that when you can't say anything, He is on the right hand of God interceding for you. He knows what you need, and He has already asked for you." Christy took her hand and said, "Jenny can I pray for you right now?"

"I would like that," Jenny replied.

"Dear Lord, I lift my friend Jenny to You. She has had so many things happening to her in the last few months and she needs You in her life. Please comfort her in the loss of Mark and may her friend Anita know Your loving care as well. We pray that the pain they're both dealing with will ease in time and they can again look forward to the plans that You have for each of their lives. You know each need they face, and we pray for Your will to be done in their lives. We love You Lord. Amen." Christy lifted her head in time to see Jenny's tears falling.

Jenny's throat was closed so tightly she barely managed to whisper, "Thank you." She thought her tears were depleted but one look at the caring face of her friend brought a new batch coursing down her cheeks. "Could you find out how Anita is doing and let me know. I miss her. I want her to be okay."

"I'll see what I can find out and let you know."

The front door opened, and Christy's grandmother came out with one of Ruth's beautiful quilts. Ruth followed her out and noticed the girls.

"There you are, Jenny, I was wondering if you were going to make it home while Christy was still here," Ruth said.

"I've been here for a little while talking to Christy," Jenny said.

"I'm glad you made it back in time to visit," Ruth said to Jenny as she paused on the steps.

"Hello Jenny," Carrie Rivers stated. "Glad you got back before we have to go." "Good to see you, Mrs. Rivers," Jenny replied. "Christy don't forget to check on that song. I have to get my report in." Jenny waved and went to the door while Ruth continued to talk to Christy and her grandmother.

"Ruth, I again thank you for the wonderful job you did on this quilt. I know it's the perfect anniversary gift for my son and his wife.

"Glad you like it and when you get the next project together bring it on over. I have two more to work on, but they won't take me long."

Jenny went on inside and couldn't hear any more of the conversation. She knew both women knew she had been crying but thankfully they had not commented on it. Going into her room she turned her computer on so she could get her report in. Before going to her email, she typed in lyrics to *The God Who Stays*. She needed to hear the words to the song one more time.

She felt much better a few minutes later as she quickly finished filling out the paperwork for the report for the Extension Office. Once the report was uploaded in an email, she clicked the send button. When she returned to the living room Ruth was once again behind another quilt that she had put in that morning. This time it was a double wedding ring pattern.

"That's going to be beautiful," Jenny said as she touched the tiny stitches Ruth had already finished. "Is this the one you were just putting in this morning?

"Yes, it is for the Anderson's daughter Julie. She isn't getting married until September, so I have plenty of time to get it out before her wedding shower."

"I wish I could quilt like you," Jenny stated with admiration in her voice.

"I will teach you whenever you're ready." Ruth laughed.

"You do so much for me now."

"I love having you here, dear. How was your day? Alma called and said Tyler was riding with you today and she had packed a picnic lunch for the two of you. Hope you enjoyed it."

"Actually, it was a good day," Jenny replied with a smile. "After we finished scouting my fields, I took Tyler out to the pond by the McDonald's place. We ate our lunch out there. It was nice having someone close to my age to talk to for a change."

"I'm glad.""The only downside was how bitter he is over his injury that cost him his career. He says he wants revenge," Jenny said, finding it difficult to forget Tyler's angry words from earlier in the day. Unshed tears sparkled in her eyes."I'm not surprised, dear," Ruth said. "Put yourself in his place and you might feel the same. I wish there was something you could do or say that would help, but Tyler will have to work through his anger. All we can do is pray that God will help him find his way in the matter."

"Why do bad things happen?" Jenny questioned. "If God loves us so much why was Tyler hurt? Why did Mark have to die?"

"I can't answer that for you Jenny. I can tell you that none of us are promised tomorrow. That is the reason we need to tell others about the Lord and lead them to make decisions for God now, at this moment, not tomorrow, not next week, next month, or even next year."

"Mark, Anita and I all accepted Jesus as our Savior a couple of years ago," Jenny confessed. "Sadly, we didn't go out and tell others about Him. We thought we had all the time in the world. Now Mark is dead, I am not sure how Anita is, and me, I'm sure God would be ashamed to call me one of His own." "You know Jenny, the reason He came was because He loved us, all of us. He died on a cross at Calvary to forgive our sins. If you ask Him to forgive you, He will. If you ask Him to help you forgive yourself, He will help you with that too."

"How can you be so sure?" Jenny questioned with hope in her voice.

"Because His word says so," Ruth replied softly as she went back to quilting.

Chapter Eight

Jenny was down on her knees weeding bean plants that had shot up overnight. She couldn't help but smile at all the people that were out and about, either visiting with those working in the community garden or serving in some way. The project was one that Ruth suggested she start in the spring as part of her community service after the accident. At first, Ruth was the only one working with her other than Tyler's grandfather, who had broken the ground and rowed up the rows for planting. Slowly one by one, mostly influenced by Ruth, others had started coming by to help with the planting. Strawberries and potatoes had already been harvested. It had been fun going door to door in the small town giving members of the community some of the fruits of their labor.

She couldn't help but feel proud of the contribution she had in creating this garden. People were stopping by and talking to each other on a plot of land that the city wasn't using for anything but growing grass. Tomatoes were green on the vine, but she noticed several had begun to turn pink, it would be only a matter of days before they would have fresh tomatoes for the table. She heard one lady tell Ruth that fried green tomatoes would sure be good for the luncheon after church service tomorrow. Zucchini and yellow squash had been picked that morning along with green beans.

Ruth came over to where Jenny was working. "I just gave Betty some green tomatoes. She insists that some fried green tomatoes were just what we need for tomorrow's lunch."

Jenny laughed and said, "I heard her telling you."

"I think our project is a success in more ways than one," Ruth added. "It is wonderful to see folks out in the community again."

"Thanks for suggesting it," Jenny replied with a smile on her face.

"You're the one who convinced the council to let us use this piece of ground for the garden. You're the one who finally got so many of the community involved in planting and keeping it watered and the grass under control."

"I love watching grandmothers show their grandchildren how to garden and get the grass out without pulling up the plants. It reminds me of my grandmother and how patient she was as she taught me how to do much of what we are doing here."

"Jenny! Jenny! You've got to come and see my watermelon," a small girl about seven came running up to her. Jenny couldn't help but smile at her enthusiasm.

"Hi Mia," Jenny said. "You already have a watermelon."

"You have to come see," Mia insisted grabbing Jenny's hand pulling her toward the other side of the garden to a section where watermelon vines were growing.

Mia pointed at a small watermelon that was about the size of a large orange. "That one is mine. See the sign there by the vine. It has Mia on it saying it is my watermelon."

"Yes, I see your name." Jenny said.

"It's going to grow and grow and grow!" Mia exclaimed. "I think it will be the biggest one in the patch."

"It is certainly looking good now."

Mia's mother walked up smiling at her young daughter and Jenny. "I just have to say thank you, Jenny, for all of this. It is so wonderful to see this town alive again. Neighbors are helping each other, they're visiting and talking, and our young folks are learning how to plant and grow their own garden."

"I hope this is just the beginning and it will be an even bigger success in the future," Jenny replied.

Jenny walked over to her jeep and got her camera out and started taking pictures. The flowers planted in triangle boxes built on each corner of the rectangle garden added color to the pictures. Mia was showing her watermelon to someone else, so she took a picture and promised herself she would take others to document the watermelon's growth. The idea for a community calendar took shape in her mind so she spent another half hour taking pictures.

Tyler and his grandfather had stopped by to check on the tomato plants that Thomas had donated to the garden. Jenny took several pictures of the two of them with Miss Ruth before they realized she was there. Tyler smiled at her.

"Granddad wanted to stop by and check on the garden," he said. "Miss Ruth was showing us how well these tomatoes are doing."

"They'll be ready to start picking before long," Jenny replied.

"I noticed."

"The garden was a good idea, Jenny," Thomas told he. "I am glad you followed through on your idea. It certainly is making a difference in this town."

"Ruth thought of it first," Jenny said not wanting all the recognition. "She was telling me how neighbors had gardens and were always sharing what they raised. I have to agree this neighborhood garden has turned out even better than I could have ever imagined."

"What do you have planned for this afternoon?" Thomas asked.

"Nothing at the moment," Jenny said.

"Would you like to go fishing with us out at the pond?"

"Sounds like fun. What time?" Jenny liked the idea of getting to spend more time with Tyler.

"When you get finished here and are ready, come on out. We have no set time and there's plenty of shade around the pond."

"Thanks, I will see you soon."

Ruth looked over at Jenny as the two men left. "Why do I get the feeling Thomas is up to something?"

"You think he is up to something?" Jenny gave her a questioning look.

Ruth ignored the look, then said, "Let's get finished here so we can get home, and you can get ready to go fishing."

******

After following the muddy ribbon of the bayou toward the McCall's farm, Jenny turned her old yellow jeep into the driveway. Alma greeted her as she reached the screen door opening it wide for her to enter.

"Come on in, Jenny, the guys are waiting out back with the fishing poles and worms. They have the ATV ready to go."

"Hey, Mrs. McCall, are you going too?" Jenny asked, noticing she had a straw hat in her hand.

"No dear, I have some baking to do for the church luncheon tomorrow," Alma replied. "Thought you might need a hat; the sun is pretty hot today."

"Thanks, I forgot to bring one," she added smiling at Tyler's grandmother.

"You can use this old one of mine. Come on through the house, no need to walk around the side when this is much quicker."

As she walked through the kitchen there was the delicious smell of Apple Cobbler baking. It was enough to make a person's mouth water.

"It smells amazing in here." Jenny said.

"You hurry along now. Maybe there'll be some cobbler waiting on you when you get back." Alma added as she opened the back door for Jenny.

Jenny hurried out the door onto the back porch. Both Thomas and Tyler were waiting beside the ATV. Although it had only been a short time since she had gone fishing with her dad, she couldn't help the glimmer of excitement that was taking control of her. Seeing the bamboo fishing poles already in the back with red and white bobbers attached to the fishing line, caused her to remember the afternoon she had shared with her dad. Jenny was determined she would spend more afternoons with him in the future.

"You ready to catch some fish? Tyler asked.

"I am," she laughed.

"Get in the front with Gramps," Tyler pointed as he sat in the back with his leg taking up most of the room. "We can be on our way."

"Hey Jenny, glad you made it," Thomas said as he starts the ATV and headed down the path to a pond about a mile from the house. "The fish are sure to be biting today. I can feel it in my bones."

Once they reached the pond, they went to a fishing spot on the west side, so they weren't facing the sun. Jenny took the can of worms and baited her hook. She was the first one to get her line into the water. She couldn't help the satisfied grin on her face when she looked up to find Tyler staring at her.

"What?" she asked. "Do I have dirt on my face or something?"

"You bait your own hook?" The surprised look on his face indicated he thought she would ask him for help.

"Of course, my grandpa taught me how when I was eight years old. I loved going fishing with him." She didn't know the melancholy look on her face reflected how much she missed him.

"Sorry for your loss," Tyler said. "Gramps told me your grandparents died last year."

"Yeah, I still miss them. But I am thankful for the memories I have of them. They were very special to me."

"I don't want to even imagine life without mine," Tyler said.

She looked back at her fishing pole when she felt a pull on her line. The red and white bobber was completely out of sight, and she could tell by the pull on the line that the fish was hooked. She pulled a good-size bream out of the water. She had never liked taking the fish off the line but was determined not to show her dislike for that part of fishing. When Tyler reached to help, she let him without any objections. While Tyler put it in one of the ice chests they had brought with them, she quickly baited the hook and dropped her line back into the water.

The next hour was taken up with catching fish. The time went by quickly. Jenny pulled a small fish from the pond then removed it from the hook and tossed it back, deciding it was too small to keep. She looked over at where Thomas was leaning up against a tree sound asleep. She remembered her grandpa used to do the very same thing.

Placing her pole up against a tree, she went to a second cooler they had brought with them and got out a cold drink. Looking at Tyler, she held it up to see if he wanted one too. When he indicated he did with a nod and smile she got him one out before closing the lid and walking back over to where he sat.

"This was fun," she said as she handed him his drink.

"Yes, I think this is the most relaxed I've been since the accident."

Jenny felt that way as well. She couldn't very well tell him so, because then he would know how she was involved with him being hurt. It was hard to understand why she wanted so badly to have him as a friend. She knew once he figured out who she was he would not be too happy about her dishonesty and would certainly not want to have anything to do with her. *He certainly would not be a friend who stays.*

"Do you believe in miracles like those talked about in the *Bible*?" Tyler asked.

"If you're asking if I believe what the *Bible* says, yes I do," Jenny replied a little surprised by the question.

"Do you think it is possible God could have one for me?" Tyler continued. "I mean He did help the lame to walk and the blind to see. Perhaps my knee would heal, and I could take back up where I left off."

"I would say that it's possible if you believed and it was His will," Jenny said. "Have you given any thought that God may have another plan for your life? One that you haven't even thought about since you've been so centered on basketball. I for one find that life doesn't always work out the way we plan, there always seems to be detours along the way."

"This has certainly been an unexpected detour for me," Tyler answered as he looked out over the pond. "I've missed a semester of school and now I'm not likely to ever have a career playing basketball."

The disappointment that Jenny could see on his face almost made her cry. *Why does life seem so unfair sometimes?*

She spoke without thinking. "You're alive, Tyler, and you still have a shot at life, so I believe God still has something planned for yours. My grandma used to say life is not always easy and it may not always go the way we plan. Usually, we learn more from the struggles than we will ever learn if things were always easy."

There was total silence for a moment before Tyler finally asked, "What about you Jenny? What do you want to do with your life?"

"I am a senior now, so I want to graduate with my class from Hamburg High. Then I want to go to college and major in art. My grandma taught me a lot about how to draw and paint when I was young. I've found I'm not too bad at it and I've even won a few art contests. I guess I want to see if I can do more with it."

"Hey, you two, are you ready to head back to the house?" Thomas asked as he got up and stretched his arms over his head. They gathered up their things, along with their catch. In all, they had ten fish between the three of them. "We still got to clean these and get them ready to fry."

The trip back to the house didn't take long. Thomas and Tyler took the fish and went to get them ready to cook. She went inside and freshened up before helping Alma cook hush puppies and French fries. She cuts up the onions and then put baked beans on to heat. Alma had the batter ready for the fish when the guys brought it to her, and she quickly cooked the fish in the deep fryer. They were soon sitting down to their meal, and everyone was in a happy mood as they shared funny stories around the table as they ate. The rest of the evening went by much too quickly and it was soon time for Jenny to leave to go back to Miss Ruth's house. It was the best day she had had in a long time. It had been fun and relaxing for a change.

Tyler walked Jenny out to her jeep when she was ready to go. "It's been a really fun day," Jenny said. "I'm glad I was invited."

"Gramps says you work too hard and need to enjoy life more."

"What about you?" Jenny questioned. "What does your Gramps say about you having more fun?"

"He thinks I take life too seriously. Unfortunately, basketball was my fun. Now I don't know what to do to have fun. I guess you could say I ate, slept, and played basketball even in my dreams," Tyler said with a faraway look in his eyes. "I did enjoy fishing this afternoon.

"That's a start, and surely there are other things you can learn to enjoy doing."

"I asked you earlier if you thought it was possible God might have a miracle for me," Tyler said. "Guess I am not ready to give up on the dream of playing again. Do you think you might pray for me Jenny, that God might give me a miracle?"

"I already do pray for you that God's will for your life will be something wonderful and fulfilling. I will add a miracle in there, and who knows, don't count God out. Remember the *Bible* says He strengthens us. I for one believe there is nothing He can't bring to pass if it is His will. We just have to remember that His will may not always be what our will is."

"I know," Tyler said. "Take care. See you at church tomorrow."

Jenny got in her jeep and waved before fastening her seat belt and cranking the engine. Tyler was already back on the porch when she pulled away. *God, do you think you could have a miracle for Tyler? He wants so badly to play basketball again. Could you heal him, Lord? Make his knee new. If it is not your will, Lord, help him to find something that would be even better than a basketball.*

Chapter Nine

The next day turned out to be a beautiful day for the church luncheon. Jenny was up early helping Ruth get food ready to take. She was looking forward to lunch and spending more time with Tyler. The afternoon and evening the day before had been like a bonus and she couldn't wait to see him again. Once dressed, she helped Ruth get the food into her car and rode with her to church. When they arrived, men and women were retrieving food from their cars and taking it into the fellowship hall where they would meet after the service. One of the dishes she was carrying was in a crockpot, so Jenny took it over and plugged it into an electric outlet and turned it to warm.

Tables had already been set up and were ready. As Jenny looked around the room, she saw Tyler's grandmother putting desserts in one section. She was putting a coconut cake with a see-through cover out and Jenny could almost taste it. Alma's cakes were the talk of the luncheon every year. She smiled at the friendly chatter that was taking place in the room. *Surely, this was what God wanted for His people, good fellowship, and a caring attitude toward one another.*

It was later during the preaching service that the pastor really caught her attention. He was talking about a church missionary group from Texas who was visiting India and witnessing to families there about the gospel. They were visiting a family that had a teenage daughter who had been crippled since birth. The missionary's young daughter was about the same age and when she learned about the crippled girl, she kept telling her father she had to pray for her. Her father said," of course we'll pray for her. The daughter insisted, "No, Father, I must pray for her." In the end, they both prayed. After they prayed, they did not notice anything different about the girl before they left.

In the following days, the missionary's daughter kept asking her father when they would know the girl was healed. Several months went by and the missionary was talking to someone who had been to India. He was telling about this family that was preaching the word of God in his community because his daughter had been healed. It turns out that this was the same family whose daughter the missionary's daughter had prayed over.

Jenny had tears in her eyes as she thought about the faith that this young girl had that God could heal a girl who had been crippled since birth. *Why couldn't she have this kind of faith*? Her grandmother had told her stories in the *Bible* over and over that had demonstrated people's faith in God. *Lord, please help me believe like that. Will you help my faith to become like my friend Christy? No one doubts her faith.*

The words to a song that she had heard a lot over the last few months came to mind. The one who made the blind to see is moving here in front of me… The one who made the deaf to hear is silencing my every fear… I believe in you I believe in you you're the God of miracles… *Yes, Lord I believe in you, and I thank You for all you have done for me. I know it is possible that you could have a miracle for Tyler, and I pray that you will give him the grace for whatever you have planned for his life.* The rest of the service was soon over. They said an ending prayer that included a blessing on the food they were about to share. The ladies were sent back to get the lunch ready, and Jenny finally saw Tyler talking to a group of friends as she went with

Ruth to get things ready. She was helping to get ice ready for drinks when she saw him again. He took a glass of iced tea from her.

"I will save you a seat with us if you want," he said.

"Okay, I'll be able to get a plate soon," Jenny said as she continued to pour iced tea into glasses as others came by to get a drink to go with their lunch.

The lady helping her with the drinks told her to go ahead and fix her plate, and she got in line. She noticed that none of the Smiths were there. In a way that was good for her. She always felt them staring at her and sending her hateful looks when she looked their way. Willie didn't bother to hide his feelings toward her. She could only imagine what Tyler would think if he saw or heard Willie or his father going on about her.

Tyler was sitting with his grandparents and another couple. He had saved a seat for her as he said. She smiled at everyone as she took the seat beside him.

"Good to see you, Jenny," Thomas said as he smiled at her. Everyone went back to eating and talking to each other and left Tyler and Jenny to visit.

"Did you notice what the sermon was on today, Jenny?" Tyler asked and she could tell by the look in his eyes that he was excited about the message. Coming so close to the conversation they had shared the night before Jenny couldn't blame him.

"Yes, I thought about what you said last night when I heard the message today," Jenny agreed.

"I believe God might have a miracle in store for me," Tyler insisted.

"I would say that God can do anything that He wants to do. You know what it says about having the faith of a mustard seed. Have you ever seen how small a mustard seed is?" Jenny asked. "I'm paraphrasing, but in Matthew 17:20 it talks about Jesus saying, "If you have faith and say to this mountain to move then expect that mountain to move. Do you believe that Tyler? Nothing is impossible with God."

"I want to Jenny, but I don't know how to believe like that?" Tyler answered. "I trust God, I have accepted him as my Savior, but how do I gain faith that could move a mountain?"

"I think about David when he was just a boy, and he was facing the giant Goliath. How did he know God was with Him?" Jenny asked. "Then I think about what my grandma used to say, because David sought God's presence in his life above all else. He prayed to God, and He had a relationship with Him. He wrote songs to God like, Psalm 27:8 which says, When thou saidst, Seek ye my face; my heart said unto thee, Thy face, Lord, will I seek."

"I'm going to talk to my grandfather and start working on what I need to do to have a closer relationship with the Lord."

"I would say that's a beginning," Jenny stated as she gathered up her plate and glass.

They tossed away their paper plates and cups and left through the fellowship hall by a side door. Once they were outside, they noticed several people walking around in the cemetery, a few placing flowers on graves.

"Is he buried here?" Tyler asked as he looked out over the cemetery.

"Who?" Jenny asked surprised by the change of the conversation.

"Mark, the boy who died in the accident," Tyler replied. "Could we visit his grave?"

Jenny knew all too well where Mark was buried. She had visited the spot long after the funeral was over and laid flowers among the many already arrayed on his grave. She had not been allowed to go to the funeral, they said it would be too painful for the family to see her there knowing she had caused his death. So, she had hidden in the woods behind the church and watched as they came out bringing the casket to the far corner of the cemetery. They laid him to rest beside his mother who had died young when Mark and Anita had been seven. Who would have thought that ten years later Mark would die so young?

"Yes, he is buried here. Come on, I can show you where," She led Tyler toward the back side of the cemetery without speaking. The silence grew as they left the church building behind. The few people visiting graves were nowhere near where Jenny was taking Tyler. They came to a stop beside a tombstone with the name Mark Smith on it. Jenny could not help the tears that flowed down her face as she thought of her young friend. Anita, Mark and she had been friends for several years, bonded by the fact none of them had a mother around to help them navigate life. Jenny didn't realize she was crying until Tyler touched her arm and turned her toward him.

"I'm sorry Jenny, I didn't mean to upset you," Tyler said with concern in his voice.

"Mark was more than a friend, Tyler. He was like a brother to me, and I still miss him," Jenny said before Tyler did something entirely unexpected. He led her over to a concrete bench placed near the grave and sat down. Pulling her down beside him, he put his arms around her and let her cry on his shoulder. She wasn't sure how long they sat there with Tyler's arms around her, but she finally stopped crying and pulled away.

It took her several minutes before she could say anything. She wiped at her tears with her hands and tried to smile. "I must look a sight," she whispered.

You look very beautiful," he told her. Taking her hands in his, he asked, "What was he like?"

Jenny couldn't keep the smile that appeared on her face from forming as she thought of her friend. "Mark was always making people laugh. He would tell some of the funniest jokes and was always trying to pull pranks on people. When a group of us got together he would keep us all laughing until we cried. I don't know of one person who didn't love him and enjoyed being around him."

"Sounds like an amazing guy," Tyler said. "Did he know the Lord?"

"Yes, he accepted Jesus as his Savior a couple of years before the accident," Jenny said. "I guess if there is any good about his death, it would have to be that he is in Heaven and one day those of us who are saved will get to see him again."

"I'm glad that he knew the Lord. Come on, let's get back to the church building," Tyler said. "Looks like folks are getting ready to leave. Would you like to go back to our house and watch a movie? I heard grandmother saying we were watching *God's Not Dead*."

"I would like to see it, but I need to check with Miss Ruth first," Jenny replied.

Miss Ruth was placing the last of her dishes in the car when they reached her. Jenny knew she had to see she had been crying but was glad she didn't comment on it when she saw they had returned.

"There you are, I was about to come looking for you when I saw you in the cemetery and knew you were probably visiting Mark's grave."

"We did," Jenny replied. "Do you mind if I go back to Tyler's grandparents for a while?"

"No, that will be fine," Ruth said. "I'm taking a plate by for a friend of mine who didn't feel like coming today. I know she will enjoy hearing about today."

"I will bring Jenny home after we watch a movie," Tyler stated.

"You drive carefully, and don't be too late," Ruth insisted.

"Yes, ma'am," Tyler assured her.

Jenny couldn't help smiling at him when he held the door to his pickup for her and helped her up into the seat. "Thanks."

The grin on his face was enough for her to know that he was enjoying their time together. She could hardly believe that in the last few days she had gotten the chance to spend a good deal of time with him. The more she got to know him the more she liked him. Not even knowing he was going to be mad at her when he found out who she was could put a damper on her day. *This was the day the Lord had made, and she would rejoice and be glad in it.*

****

A few hours later the movie they had spent the afternoon watching, *God's Not Dead*, had just went off. Tyler's grandparents had watched it with them, and it reminded Jenny of many weekends spent with her own grandparents. Spiritual matters were an important part of the memories that she had of her time with them. She wished that her memories with her parents held remembered talks about God and worship services. Unfortunately, her family had not made sure she got the same spiritual training as they had growing up.

"That movie has a great message. Sad to say, so many people in our country have turned their backs on God," Thomas commented as the music played through to the end. "They take their electronics so seriously and spends hours on social media sites or listening to all kinds of nonsense. They'll not spend even five minutes reading a *Bible* verse or listen to a gospel message, or spending time in prayer. Then they wonder what's wrong with this country."

"I think that song *God's Not Dead* has a powerful message that says something extra ordinary can happen when you believe," Alma said. "I wish more young people would seek His presence. That they could feel the love He has for each of us. If only they would let Him in, there's no doubt that He could change their lives for the better."

"You've both always taught me truth about God. I want you to know that I am thankful and feel blessed to have grandparents like you in my life. I told Jenny today at lunch that I want to have a closer relationship with the Lord. I'm counting on both of you to help me with that goal," Tyler said.

"We are proud of you, Tyler," Thomas said as he placed his hand on his grandson's shoulder. "Glad you have the Word of God to guide you and keep you on the right path. God's Word is alive and powerful, and it changes lives for those who give their hearts to Jesus. All who will listen will have a deeper understanding of truth than those who ignore it. The plan is so simple and all you must do to be saved is to believe in Jesus. Believe He came to earth to die for our sins, believe He died on the cross at Calvary and three days later He arose from the grave and is in Heaven making intercession for those who love Him."

"I am glad of your guidance," Tyler said.

"Thanks for letting me share the movie with all of you today," Jenny said as she helped clean up by taking the popcorn bowls to the kitchen.

"Glad you could come over," Alma said. "We enjoyed having you here and come back anytime you get a chance."

Even with his crutches, Tyler moved ahead to open the door for Jenny as she walked outside. It was a lot warmer as they walked toward the truck than it had been when they arrived. When they reached the truck Tyler again opened the door for Jenny. After closing the door, he moved slowly around to the drivers' side, putting his crutches behind his seat before getting in.

Looking over at Jenny as he cranked the truck, he said, "I was thinking about what granddad said after the movie. When you think about there being no place on earth that has access to know the Lord as we do here in America, yet so many know nothing about Jesus and what He did for mankind."

"Yeah, I know what you mean," Jenny replied. "Many problems are facing us today, but none that are as important as the soul of our country. Lately, I have seen people get angry if someone even mentions the name Jesus Christ or talks about the message of the cross. I'm not sure why they are so angry about someone telling them about God. They have a choice of not listening if they don't want to. Why are they so angry? I can't seem to get my head around that question."

"We live in a broken world, Jenny," Tyler answers. "Many people are suffering. They live in poverty surrounded by violence, they're in pain and they see no way out of a cycle that offers little hope. Then some Christian comes along and tells them all they need is Jesus. Because we're saved, we have God's Spirit to empower us to assure us of His presence in this life and for all eternity. Most people don't have that. They find it hard to accept, they are angry someone has the audacity to tell them about this man Jesus that can make all their problems go away."

"That's just it. They want to know if there is a God why He would let certain things happen. Just because we are Christians it doesn't mean that we won't have troubles in our life. It just means that when we trust in the Lord, we have spiritual resources that help us to deal with whatever life sends our way."

"Like the accident that took away my career," Tyler said. "God has seen me through some tough moments since I got hurt. I've still got a long way to go, especially when dealing with this anger I have toward the person who caused the accident."

"Do you think you will be able to forgive them?" Jenny asked.

"Right now, I can't," Tyler replied. "One day maybe, but not right now."

"Then I will pray you will one day find it in your heart to forgive them." Jenny could only hope he would one day forgive her. She knew he was going to be so angry with her once he knew who she was. She also knew she needed to tell him, but worried he would hate her once he learned the truth. Not tonight, she couldn't do it tonight.

Chapter Ten

"Date?" Thomas asks his grandson as he comes out the front door.

"Jenny and I are going to meet a college friend of mine at the rodeo arena in Hamburg to watch some high school rodeo practice." Tyler said with a grin.

"That's good son, glad you're getting out and taking Jenny along. Don't think she gets out much."

The sound of a truck pulling up in the driveway had them both looking in that direction. A new shiny black Club Cab Chevy stopped in front of the house. The driver got out and took his time coming up to the front steps.

"Thomas, Tyler, glad I caught you both at home," Ted Smith said. "I would like to take a few minutes of your time."

"What's on your mind, Ted?" Thomas asked.

"That Reynolds girl," he said angrily. "Both Tyler and I have a decision to make. I hope to persuade him in helping me see she gets what is coming to her."

"How's that?" Tyler questioned not liking the attitude of the large man standing on the sidewalk leading to the front steps.

"I have my attorney working on getting her tried as an adult. He is going to try and talk her into taking a deal where we don't even have to go to court just sign some papers. My family will get the Reynolds place and it's up to you, boy, what you want to ask for. My attorney tells me she can only go to the facility until she is 18, not nearly long enough. So far, she is turning this plan down. But if she is tried as an adult, she could get a lot of time in the slammer, and it makes the deal more attractive if she could be locked up for a long time. With the farm and cash settlement from her grandparents I'm ready to put this behind me. My family and I need to get on with our lives, but until she spends some time locked up, I can't let it go."

"What makes you think she is going to accept being locked up till she is 18?" Tyler asked.

"She will listen to her attorney if she knows what is good for her. Going to trial facing it as an adult should put the right pressure on her." Ted said. "I hope you will talk to your attorney and work with mine to see this thing gets done."

"I've not decided exactly what I am going to agree to, but I am meeting with my attorney in a few days, and I will have to get back to you." Tyler replied, a bitter taste in his mouth once more as he thought of what was still ahead of him. He didn't really want to go to court but he did want justice. What he wanted, even more, was a full story of the events of that night. Maybe then he could come to terms with what life had handed him.

"How is Anita doing?" Thomas questioned.

"Not good. I don't think I have ever seen anyone so sad and lifeless. She stills feels sorry for that little fool who killed my son."

"They were friends for a lot of years, Ted. This must be doubly hard on her," Thomas said.

"I just wish her mother was still alive. She would know what to do to help her. Me, I'm not having much luck in that area."

"What about Susan's mother, Anita's grandmother?" Thomas asked. "She lives close enough I know she would help."

"That's not going to happen." Ted stated. "She's a busybody and all she does is cause more problems."

"I'm sorry you feel that way, Ted," Thomas added. "Personally, I believe Louise is a good Christian woman that would do anything necessary to help her grandchildren."

"Just a little too much preaching for my taste," Ted insisted.

"Time has a way of healing things," Thomas said.

"No amount of time is going to make this better. We'll all be better when that girl is locked up," Ted said as he stepped away from the porch steps. "Let me know what you decide." They watched him walk back down the sidewalk until he got in his truck and left.

"Tyler, there is something I need to talk to you about…" Thomas begins. "It'll have to wait, Gramps. I am going to be late getting Jenny, and we still need to drive to Hamburg. I want to get there before practice is over." He was already going down the steps using his crutches with care. He knew his grandfather was watching him make his way to his truck.

"Okay, but we have to talk first thing in the morning about Jennifer Reynolds." His grandfather called out before he reached the end of the sidewalk.

Tyler turned around to look back at his grandfather before saying, "You're going to try and change my mind about what I have to do. I get it, Gramps, that's who you are. This is my decision to make."

"The question is are you planning to get justice or decide justice?"

"Is there a difference?"

"Yes, there's a big difference," he replied. "Smith has decided to get revenge. Justice has nothing to do with his war on this young girl."

Tyler stared at his grandfather almost speechless for a moment. He finally said, "She was driving drunk and killed his son, Gramps. She took my career. Doesn't that require payment?"

"If it was an accident…" Thomas started to say when Tyler cut him off.

"An accident that should never have happened," Tyler insisted as he faced his grandfather. "She has to face the responsibility of drinking and driving."

"I'm sorry. I didn't mean to upset you. Go have some fun with your friends and we will talk again tomorrow." Thomas watched his grandson move slowly down the sidewalk out to his truck. Alma came to stand beside him and put her arms around him.

"You know we have to tell him," Alma said. "He isn't going to be very happy about us not telling him Jenny and Jennifer are the same person."

"I know," Thomas replies.

Tyler left his grandparents standing on the porch with a feeling that they were keeping something from him. For one thing, they seem to side with this Jennifer Reynolds whenever her name came up. Just that morning, he had almost walked in on his grandmother and some lady named Grace, when they were having an argument over the same girl. Grace was talking about her and his grandmother was defending her. He had not heard all they said but enough to know who they were talking about.

The woman called Grace had been saying, "Can you believe she showed up at church Sunday. She's trying to get on the good side of everyone before going to court. I know Ted is working on seeing she gets what she deserves."

"Grace, she has been going to our church for a long time. She came with her grandparents." His grandmother had told her.

Tyler didn't remember seeing anyone at church on Sunday that might have been her. Of course, he had little attention other than for Jenny, so he wasn't sure if he saw her or not. He had walked away without listening to any more of the conversation. Both his grandparents had good hearts and tried to live a life for Christ. He knew they cared about the girl that had caused the accident that had injured him so badly. That was the reason his grandfather had said they would talk tomorrow. They were going to make sure whatever he did in court was what God would want him to do. He already knew it was not necessarily what he wanted from the human standpoint of getting even for the harm done. He already knew an eye for an eye was not the settlement they would want for him.

As he pulled up in front of the house where Jenny was living, he forced himself to forget about what he still had to face. It could wait till another day. Getting out of the truck he used his crutches to get up the doorsteps to the front door. He knocked on the door and heard a dog barking from inside before the door was opened by a short elderly lady.

"You must be Tyler," she said with a smile.

"I am here to get Jenny," he said, returning her smile.

"Jenny! Your young man is here."

Jenny heard the dog barking and knew Tyler had arrived to pick her up for their date. She thought Tuesday would never get here but the day had finally arrived. She had been up at the crack of dawn and visited all her fields by noon. She spent the afternoon getting ready. The biggest problem she faced was what to wear from a wardrobe that didn't leave a lot to choose from. She finally picked out a long loose-fitting light blue cotton blouse over a tank top and blue jean legging. White tennis shoes and a white handbag completed her outfit.

Taking out dangling silver earrings with tiny navy-blue stars attached from a small jewelry box she put them in her ears. After adding a light coat of lipstick, she stepped back from the mirror and gazed at her reflections. The light blue top was perfect for her shoulder-length strawberry blond hair she decided to leave down. When she walked into the living room Tyler was dressed in a light blue button-up shirt opened at the neck with blue jeans and cowboy boots. She knew her choice of clothes was good when she saw the pleased look on his face.

"Hey Jenny," he said. "Are you ready?"

"I am," she said. Turning to Miss Ruth she added, "We shouldn't be late."

"You have your key?" Ruth asked. Holding up her handbag she smiled before going out the door ahead of Tyler. He was a little slower, so she didn't rush to the truck and was glad she didn't when he moved ahead, opened the door for her, and waited for her to get in before closing it. She watched him move around to the driver's side and put his crutches behind his seat before getting in.

"So, where are we going?" Jenny asked as Tyler started the truck and backed out into the street. "To a rodeo practice," he laughed. "My friend, Matt's dad has gotten permission to use the arena so a lot of the high school rodeo competitor can practice. A couple of my friends are going to Nationals including Matt's little brother. Billy is a bronco rider, and my friend Stacy is a barrel racer. We should get to see both Billy and Stacy ride this afternoon and evening."

"Sounds like fun," Jenny agreed. "I've been to a few rodeos."

"Sit back and relax. It shouldn't take long," Tyler said turning up the radio to a County Western station and started singing along with most of the songs.

The time passed quickly, and in under thirty minutes they were taking a side street off the main highway to the Ashley County Fairgrounds before reaching their destination.

Jenny asked, "This is the Hamburg Riding Club arena?"

"We're almost there. It is out behind the fairground buildings."

As they turned onto another street, they drove around to the back where other vehicles were parked. Jenny knew there would be people here at this event that knew her. They might say something that would let Tyler know who she was. She wondered if the Stacy he mentioned was a classmate of hers. Several trucks with horse trailers were parked off to the side away from the parking lot they were heading for. Several girls were riding and warming up their horses in the area around the parked trailers. Tyler continued around them and found a place to park his truck that was closer to the arena.

There were a lot of cars and trucks parked there. Tyler's friend must have been watching for him because almost as soon as Tyler stepped out of the truck someone came up behind him and took him in a big bear hug and was slapping him on his back. Jenny gave the two friends a moment before going around the truck to join them.

"Man, I can't believe you are finally here," his friend was saying.

"Matt, this is Jenny," Tyler said introducing her.

"Good to meet you Jenny," Matt gripped her hand in a firm handshake. He stared at her for a moment. "You look familiar. Have we meet before?"

Jenny's heart accelerated for a moment thinking he might remember her from some of the newspaper articles from a few months before. She quickly said, "I don't think so. Tyler tells me we are going to see some rodeo action."

"Yeah, the girls are about to start barrel racing in a few minutes. Come on and we will find a place in the stands so we can watch the action," Matt said leading the way toward the stands. He slowed his pace so Tyler could keep up with him.

"Your dad still over seeing practices?" Tyler asked as they reached the bleachers and took a seat about three rows up.

"You know he is," Matt stated. "He has slowed down a little but with Billy bronco riding he is here every practice. My parents are on the road to wherever Billy is riding. We're all planning to be at Nationals in Colorado in a few weeks.

"That's great." Tyler said with envy in his voice, wishing he could be there too.

They had just sat down when a voice over the loudspeaker announced the barrel racing was about to begin. The barrels had already been placed in the arena and the first rider was getting ready to go.

Alright folks, we are ready for our first rider from Crossett, Mattie Turner. A small blond-haired girl raced into the arena and proceeded to round the barrels in a clover leaf pattern. The seconds ticked off on the display clock for everyone to see and moments later the first time was posted at 16.3 seconds. The next two riders Carrie Walker and Mandy Norman, also from Crossett area, proceeded in the same pattern with the first one scoring 16.8 seconds and the other 16.6 seconds. All three riders looked amazing to Jenny.

When the announcer introduced the next rider, it was obvious there was something different in the atmosphere. "Let's give a hometown welcome to our very own Stacy Connor ladies and gentlemen from right here in Hamburg." In the stands everyone clapped, and several young men whistled.

A moment later a beautiful red head raced out of the tunnel into the arena on a chocolate-colored quarter horse with a white blaze down his face. Both horse and rider move as one tightly racing around the first barrel then flew across the arena in a figure-eight rounding the second barrel. The pair continued to the third barrel again tightly racing around it before riding like the wind back out through the tunnel. The time recorded was 15.7 seconds.

"There you are, folks, the best time of the night by Stacy Connor. The crowd again clapped and whistled for the last rider. Three more girls rode but no one else came close to Stacy's time. "Let's give all our girls a round of applause." A few moments later everyone had settled back down.

Jenny noticed new activity in the arena. A truck was driven into the arena to pick up the barrels. Calf roping came next, followed a little while later by steer wrestling. Once that was over, they were finally getting ready for the bronco riding event. There were five guys lined up near the chutes with one already getting in position for the first ride. Out in the arena, two horses with pick-up riders had entered to help each bronco rider dismount after his ride. The gate was opened, and the first rider and horse were in the air as the horse bucked and twisted and tried to unseat the rider on his back. The young cowboy leaned back and stayed on until the eight second buzzer sounded. A few moments later the pick-up riders moved into place to get him off the horse.

Jenny didn't realize she was squeezing Tyler's arm until the first rider was off his horse and back on the ground. Tyler laughed at her. "That was intense," he said reaching over and holding her hand during the rest of the rides. The next thirty minutes went by quickly. Several people came by and spoke to Tyler in between one rider finishing and another getting ready for the next ride.

"Aren't you glad there are no bull riders today," Tyler laughed.

"More like, aren't you?" she replied. "You may have bruises tomorrow."

"Tyler! Tyler McCall! Is that really you," the young redheaded girl came running up the steps and gave Tyler a big hug. "Did you see me ride?"

"I did," Tyler said with a laugh. "Stacy, you were amazing."

"I'm going to Nationals! And so is Billy!" she exclaimed. Her excitement was certainly understandable after the way she had ridden just a short time before.

"I'm proud of you," Tyler added his arm still around the girl as they stood side by side.

"What's she doing here?" Stacy demanded as her eyes came to rest on Jenny. There was no doubt she knew exactly who Jenny was and she was about to tell Tyler.

It took Tyler a few minutes to realize that Stacy was talking about his date. Jenny stepped back, the smile on her face quickly fading. She stared down at her feet not wanting to see the look on Tyler's face knowing how much of a shock he was about to receive.

"Tyler, what are you doing here with Jennifer Reynolds?" Stacy's declared her temper matching her red hair. Jenny couldn't blame her. After all, it was obvious, she loved Tyler. It was there in the possessive way she still stood with her arm around his back. "She's the person responsible for your injuries. How could you bring her here?"

Tyler looked stunned, standing motionless in the middle of the stands surrounded by his friends. The wounded expression in his eyes was quickly turning livid and she knew his anger was all toward her, and she realized their short friendship had just come to an end.

"You're Jennifer Reynold?" He demanded making no secret of the fact he detested her now and felt that she had tricked him.

Jenny flinched, but her pride quickly came to her aide. She would not let her humiliation show in front of all these people. After all, it was her own fault she had been found out. Trying her best to keep her composure, she quickly turned and walked away. Her heart felt as if it was breaking into a million pieces, but she would not let tears fall. Pausing for a moment she turned back, and her eyes met his,

"I'll wait for you at the truck," she said before walking away. She slowly made her way back to Tyler's truck and leaned against it. How did things go so wrong in less than sixty seconds? One moment she was having so much fun and moments later it was all over.

The rodeo practice continued as if nothing had just happened to change the way Tyler would now look at her. She was dreading him coming back to the truck. If she had another way home, she would have taken it. She would not call someone else to come get her, it was her own fault she was in this situation, and she would face Tyler's anger. The sooner the better as far as she was concerned, or at least that was what she kept telling herself. She wasn't sure how much time passed, maybe a half hour before she saw him slowly making his way across the parking lot and she saw his face.

He looked sad and hurt but didn't speak to her as he took out his keys and unlocked the door. Their eyes met for a brief second before hers dropped, and she went around and got in without saying a word.

What could she say? How could she explain? She couldn't and there was no reason to try. She knew he hated her.

Tyler climbed in and cranked the engine without saying a word. A lot of the cars and trucks were beginning to leave or had already gone. He was able to pull forward and take the road back out to the main highway. She was not even sure how much time passed before he pulled into a convenience store and got out and began pumping gas. Jenny went inside to the restroom and picked up a soft drink. The bell over the door jingled as Tyler came inside. He looked at her across the store then turned and walked toward the restroom. She gave him a few minutes before heading to the counter. She looked over at a young boy who was waiting to be checked out in front of her. He was saying, "Look Mommy, that's the lady in the paper."

Jenny's smile failed as she saw the headlines across the local newspaper that was on the counter. Tyler walked up and looked at her and back at the paper as if he couldn't believe his eyes. The look on his face was one of saying no this couldn't be happening again in less than an hour. He picked up the paper, laid it on the counter, and told the checker he was paying for her drink. He never said a word to her, just paid and walked out the door. Jenny followed behind but was in no hurry to walk outside. She didn't know what Tyler's reaction was going to be, but from the look he had just given her she was in no hurry to find out.

Tyler's accusing gaze became fixed on Jenny as she stepped out the door. His handsome features seem to be frozen and the bitterness she had seen in him the first day she met him was back. He looked so forbidding.

"Please Tyler, I know this is a shock," she tried to explain.

"Don't …" he said coldly.

"Please give me a …" A sob broke her voice as she pleaded for him to understand.

"Chance!" Tyler jeered. "What were you figuring on? That I would become so besotted with you I'd drop charges?"

"No!" she said softly. "I knew you would never have anything to do with me if you knew who I was."

"That's probably the first true statement to come out of your mouth since I've meet you," he said forcefully, his eyes coldly accusing as he starred at her.

"Tyler, I can't undo …"

"Exactly! There is no reason for you to try. Get in the truck and I'll take you home, and then I hope I never have to see or speak to you again." His limp was hardly noticeable as long strives took him across the parking lot to his truck. He wasn't using his crutches, and she wonders if he even noticed. The door was yanked open, and he got inside and slammed it shut.

Moving on faltering legs she followed the path Tyler had made and opened the passenger door and slid into the truck seat. Silence filled the cab, and she acknowledged to herself that it would do little good to attempt to reach the rigid figure beside her. She fastened her seat belt without looking over at him. The distance between them seemed like miles instead of the few inches that separated them in the small space. She had no one to blame but herself. She had known the day would come when he would find out who she was. She just wasn't ready for it to be today.

Jenny lifted her chin. Her pride would not let him see her cry. She had felt this kind of pain before and being alone had become part of her reality. She felt this way when her mother left and did not return. Again, when her grandparents passed away and her father had been in a hospital. Most recently when Mark had been killed and Anita and all her friends were no longer speaking to her. She had felt pain the day of the hearing and no family member had shown up, but Ruth had stepped up and taken her home. She had survived then, and she would now. She didn't recall the twenty-mile ride to Wilmot, but when the truck stopped in front of Ruth's house, she was out the door and heading inside without speaking. She heard the squealing of his tires on the pavement, but she never looked back.

She wiped the tears running down her face and took several deep breaths before entering the house. The light was on in the kitchen, but Ruth was already in bed. Jenny was thankful. She wasn't up to seeing her right now. Locking the front door and turning off lights, she moved down the hall on leaden feet. She just wanted to crawl into bed and stay there forever. She didn't remember getting ready for bed, but once there she drowned her pillow in tears. Once the tears started it was like a dam had broken and it was a very long time before she cried herself out.

Chapter Eleven

Jenny was up early the next morning and decided to check boll weevil traps since it was a Wednesday. She had slept little the night before and had to use makeup to help cover up some of the damage. If things had been different, she would have asked Tyler to go with her again today and then over to her dad's. Those days were over, and she was back to being alone once again. Who needed friends anyway?

She was almost finished with her last traps when she heard loud pipes on a pickup racing up the road. The vehicle had loud music thumping and several boys riding in the back shouting and laughing at each other. She waited until they passed by since she was in a corner of a field hidden by trees and bushes that had grown up next to the road. Taking the opposite direction onto the main road she took the long way back in hopes of not running into Willie and his friends. She had almost reached the road into McCall's home place when Willie came roaring up behind her. Trying to ignore him she continued toward town not wanting to be stranded in an area without other people around with Willie and his bunch of friends.

Willie kept pulling up beside her and easing his vehicle almost into her causing her to slow down. When she did that, he did too, and if she sped up, he did that also. Pulling out her phone she started recording what was going on and turned on her CB and requested help. She knew she sounded frightened but once he realized what was going on, he hit her right front wheel and forced her off the road into a ditch.

Willie jumped out and grabbed the phone and erased the video. "You think you're so smart. I've got witnesses, this never happened. You're going to pay for killing my brother. Your days of walking around like you didn't do anything is about to come to an end. Everyone will think you're just trying to get attention before going to court by this little action," he laughed. He tossed the phone into the ditch before jumping back into his truck and taking off. She saw him take a side road. A few minutes later the sheriff Bob Warren and her father pulled up beside where her jeep sat in the ditch.

"Jenny, are you okay?" Bob Warren asked.

"Yeah, I am now," she said walking down the ditch to find her phone. "Do you think you could help me get my jeep out?

Her father went over and got in. He put it in four-wheel drive and had it out within minutes.

"Jenny, what happened here?" her dad asked.

"Willie and his friends were running his vehicle up beside me and backing off. I started videoing what they were doing, and he ran me off the road. He took my phone, erased the video, and tossed it in the ditch. Willie said he had witnesses who would say this never happened. Then they took off down that road over there."

"Bob, what can we do about this?" "I'll have a talk with Willie and his father. If Jenny wants to press charges, we can fill out paperwork. I intend to let Willie know he must stay away from her. I'll make sure Ted understands the seriousness of all of this as well."

"I really don't want to press charges. Things are bad enough for his family." Jenny said. "Willie is just being a bully. Besides he has witnesses that will say he didn't do anything. No one will believe me."

"Bob?" her father started. "Your daughter is right. He has witnesses and she was by herself. But I'll have a talk with Ted all the same and let him know this had better not continue." Bob explained. "I'm still writing this up, so we'll have it on file in case he does something else. You don't have to file anything at this time, I'll just write it in my report on this call. I promise you I will follow up with Willie and his dad on this and I'll inform other officers in the area to be diligent on this."

"Thanks for letting me come with you on the call, but I'm going to finish the ride with Jenny," her father said.

"Okay, I'll see you tomorrow and we'll see if we can get that sunroom enclosed and the rest of the windows in."

"Thanks for your help." Jenny said to the sheriff.

"Jenny you be careful out here by yourself scouting these fields. Report anything else that Willie and his friends do." Bob walked back to his car and got in and pulled away.

Jenny's dad got in the passenger's seat and waited for her to crank up the engine. She went down and turned around at the next side road Willie and his friends had taken.

"I only have four more traps to check, and I will be finished today," she said. "I was almost to the drive to the McCall's place when Willie showed up behind me. I was afraid to turn off. I didn't want to be caught in an area that someone else might not come along. I wasn't sure what Willie might do. The bayou runs through there close to the road."

"That was smart, Honey," her father said. "Glad Bob and I had started into town to get some supplies when the call came in you needed help."

"I did wonder how you got here so quickly," she said. Turning down the McCall's road she drove pass the place where Tyler had run her off the road and on around by the house and to the fields behind.

She quickly took care of the four traps left for her to check. The likelihood of Willie and his friends bothering her again today didn't worry her, but having her father along made her feel much better.

"Would you like to come back to the house and meet Miss Ruth while I get my report sent in?" Jenny asked. "Then I can run you home and see what's been happening there."

"Make sure to bring clothes to paint in, you can help me paint the porch," he said. "We can run by that Burger Shack and get some food on the way back through town."

Once they reached Ruth's house Jenny introduced the two and left them talking while she ran in and got her report typed up and uploaded it in an email. When she pushed send, she got out a small bag and put a change of clothes inside. It would be good to get to spend a little time with her dad.

Ruth gave them some fried apple pies she had made that morning to go with their lunch. Ruth hugged Jenny and said, "Go enjoy time with your dad."

"Love you, Miss Ruth," Jenny whispered, again fighting back tears. Seemed all she wanted to do lately was cry. "I'll be home before dark."

"I love you too," she replied. "God bless you child and keep you safe."

"Ruth seems like a good person," her dad said as they were getting in the jeep.

"Ruth is a true Christian, Dad. If someone wanted to see an example of one, she should be the picture. She taught me the word Christian means "a partisan for Christ." She said she read it somewhere. That means being committed to Christ, confessing your sins, asking for forgiveness, and then living for Him as your Lord and Savior."

"She's right. I know your grandmother thought a lot of Ruth. They were best friends back before I left and joined the Marine Corp," he said. "Something your grandmother use to say to me was the lost world doesn't see God, but they can see God's children. The things you see in Christians are the things people will believe about God. Ruth is a good example of that, and I think it is the reason she helped you when you needed someone to step up."

"I'm very thankful for her, Dad. She saved me that day in court. She has been there for me every day since."

"I'm sorry your mother and I haven't been here for you, Honey," he said with regret in his voice. "Maybe someday I can make up for being gone so much of your life."

"Dad, I know you were serving our country, and I feel you were doing your part to keep all of us safe," Jenny said. "Yeah, I missed you not being here a lot. But the world we live in today, we need good men and women looking out for us. I just wish you could have been around more."

Jenny pulled up to the Burger Shack. Her dad had ordered their burgers just before they left Ruth's house, so he went in to get them. The talk with her dad surprised her. He listened and heard what she had to say. Her life was a mess, but if her father could fight his way out of his problems of only a few weeks ago, she could do the same. After all, she was her father's daughter.

The burgers smelled great when he got back in the vehicle. "Wow, I can't wait to get home and eat," she laughed. "Let's hurry, I know what you mean." The drive out to the home place didn't take long and they quickly got out of the jeep to go inside. "You can't look around until we have eaten, so go directly to the kitchen," her dad said.

She noticed he had finished the floors in the hallway. She liked it. He had gone with the darker flooring after all. She was glad, it looked amazing. Arriving in the kitchen she was shocked by the difference in the room. New floor tile had been put in and countertops had been replaced with new counters. There was now an island in the middle with bar stools on one side. This is where they placed the burgers, and her father handed her paper plates to put her meal on. They took a seat, and her father took a moment to bow his head and say thanks for the meal.

Taking the burger out of the bag, Jenny could hardly wait to take a bite. "If this tastes as good as it looks," she started taking a bite. "Hum. This is even better."

"I'll have to agree but I have already had one of the burgers, so I already know how good it is," her dad laughed. "The fries are special too."

Jenny tasted her fries and again had to agree with her dad's assessment. "They were delicious."

"Now, I am wondering why I haven't tried Burger Shack before," Jenny said. "I would have one of these every day."

"Maybe because that wasn't the name of the place and the new cook only started this past week," Dave replied. "He is a friend of mine from the Marine Corps. He's had a tough time, like me, adjusting to being out of the Corps. I'm giving him a place to stay and he's working at the food place part-time and helping me with getting this place back in shape."

"That's good, you have someone to help you," Jenny said. "Dad, do you think mom ever thinks of us?"

"I can't answer that, Honey. I don't even know where your mom is."

"It's been a long time since I have received any mail from her," Jenny replied. "I would never have thought she would just up and leave without saying where she was going. But she did. I know she talked to grandma about it, but never told me anything. She just promised that she loved me, and she was going to make a difference in the world before walking out the door."

"Where did the letters come from?"

"Washington, DC."

"Really? Wonder what she was doing there?"

"I don't know. At first, she wrote often but then about once a week. Letters stopped coming altogether about a year ago around the time grandpa and grandma got sick," Jenny said. "I haven't received any mail for over a year. She never contacted me by phone or internet, so I don't have a phone or an email address."

"Look, I still have some contacts. I might be able to find something out. I'll keep you posted," he said. "Now, do you want to see what's been accomplished in four weeks?"

"Yes, I do," she laughed. "Where do we start?"

"Let me show you the upstairs first since there was so much damage to the ceilings in two of the bedrooms." He led the way up the stairs Jenny couldn't believe the results in such a short time. Weeks before she was placing pans under the leaks in the ceiling, now you could see no sign that it ever leaked. "This is amazing. How did you do this so quickly?"

"I've had a lot of help. As you know Bob has been helping since we replaced the roof. A couple of his deputies are coming over and helping when they have time. My friend, the cook, has been here for a couple of weeks helping with painting and much of the cooking. Come on, let me show you what the living area looks like. The floor is almost finished in there and we're going to get someone to come in and put a wood insert in the fireplace to make heating more efficient."

The walls in the living room were painted with the light cream they had picked out the first day. Jenny felt a little disappointed she had missed out on so much of the work and time with her dad. She also noticed the change in him. He seemed happier and more like he used to be. Maybe the home place had been what he needed to get his mind off his injuries and give him something else to think about. Then she noticed the double doors leading out of the room onto a sunroom that had been added.

"Dad, is this the new sunroom?" she asked opening the door and walking into a room that ran the whole length of the back of the house. "It is beautiful." Tears came to her eyes when she thought of how her grandmother would have loved it. "Grandma would have loved this."

"All we like in here is finishing up with painting and installing the rest of the windows before we tile it like we did the kitchen. You want to help me finish the painting up in here?"

"Dad, I love it and yes, I want to help."

"Go get your painting clothes on." He laughed. Jenny loved the sound of his laughter, and it reminded her of better times.

Chapter Twelve

Tyler tossed the paper on the breakfast table with the picture of Jennifer Reynolds on the cover. He looked at both his grandparents. That he wanted answers was written all over his face. Despite his hurt feelings about his family lying to him, he would give them a chance to explain why. He stayed silent for several moments waiting to see what they would say. Finally, when it looked as if they weren't going to respond he asked, "Why have you been keeping this from me? You had to know that I didn't know Jenny and this Jennifer was the same person. What I don't understand is why you didn't tell me?"

"That first day, you were such an angry young man. You had already convicted Jenny and judged her," his grandmother said. "We both thought if you got to know her you would see a young girl who is hurting and in need of a friend. I am sorry that you found out this way instead of Jenny or us telling you. Now, what do you plan to do? Are you going to get your attorney to join Ted Smiths to see she's locked up?"

"She doesn't belong behind bars, this I am absolutely sure of," Thomas said. "Jenny is one of the sweetest young girls that I know. She's so much like her grandmother, I just can't stand the idea that she might have to go to a correction facility till she is eighteen, or worse, tried as an adult and spend years behind bars."

"The other thing we're concerned with is she may have been the one to cause the accident. I don't know. Could she have also been the one who saved your life?" Alma asked. "I'm sure you haven't given any thought to that?"

"What do you mean?" Tyler questions with a surprised look on his face.

"Who pulled you out of that burning car Tyler? Someone did," Alma said.

"Maybe you should read the reports and ask some questions. You were out of the car lying beside Jenny on the ground. As you know it caught fire before help arrived. There was no one else there except Jenny and Anita that could have gotten you out. Maybe they both helped you; I don't know. Jenny nor Anita will talk to anyone about that night. I just find it strange that neither girl will say anything." Thomas said.

"I know it must be painful to remember your brother or friend dying. I'm not surprised they don't want to talk about it. That's not such a big mystery." Alma insisted.

"I've started having some memories that come and go, but nothing concrete. I haven't thought about who got me out. I just thought it must have been the police or firemen who responded to the accident," Tyler said, and for the first time considering there might be more to the story than he had first thought.

"Glad you said accident," his grandmother said. "Why does no one consider that it was just that, an accident?"

"Tyler, I think you care about this young girl. Don't let your pride ruin your relationship with her." Thomas said watching the reaction of his grandson.

"She lied to me," Tyler replied. "You can't have a relationship based on lies."

"Do you remember in the *Bible* when Jesus said to the crowd, he who has no sin should cast the first stone?" his grandfather asked. "Do you recall what happened next?"

"Yes, I know no one would pick up a stone and throw it," Tyler replied. "Yes, I do know why no one could do it."

******

Shortly after lunch, Tyler decided he would go visit the Smiths. Earlier in the day he had called his attorney to see if he had a copy of the police report. He did, so he had him email him a copy. His grandparents had been right about there being no one at the accident scene when the police arrived but Mark, who was dead, Anita, his twin sister, Jenny, and him. He had sat for a long time thinking about if Jenny was the one who had pulled him from the car. That would mean she saved his life. That would really put a new spin on things. Would Anita tell him what she knew?

When Tyler pulled up at the Smith's house, he was glad that Ted Smith big black pickup wasn't in the driveway. Maybe he wasn't home. The first thing that Willie said to him when he answered the door was, "If you're here to talk to my dad, he isn't here. He won't be back till late."

"I was wondering if I could talk to Anita." Tyler said.

"Not sure that would be a good idea without dad being here," Willie said a frown on his face. Was that an expression of alarm? Willie looked back inside, took a deep breath and in a low voice said, "She isn't having a very good day."

"What do you mean I'm not having a very good day? Who are you talking to Willie?" Anita Smith asked as she came out of the living room. "You're Tyler McCall. Would you like to come in?"

"Well, I …" Tyler started to step through the door.

"Wait a minute," Willie said, putting his arm across the doorway holding the door from being open any further.

"Don't worry Willie, Dad was expecting Tyler to come over. Didn't he tell you?" Anita said sharply.

"Yeah, but not while he isn't here." Willie repeated. "I'm sure he wouldn't be too happy about him being here when he isn't."

"Tyler, would you care for a glass of lemonade out on the patio. That way you won't be in the house without him here," Anita giggled. "Willie will show you around to the patio, while I get us some refreshments."

Willie gave Tyler a blank look for a moment after Anita walked away. He was used to getting what he wanted, and he seemed taken aback that his sister had just invited Tyler to stay. Willie pulled the door closed and started leading the way around the house. That he was mad wasn't hard to read by his body language. Once they reached the patio, he pointed at a chair for Tyler to sit in.

"I'm warning you now, don't you dare upset her with your nosey questions," Willie said, all signs of being friendly gone. He took out his phone and started texting someone. "I'm not stupid, I know why you're here."

"It's not my intentions to upset your sister," Tyler said wondering why Willie was so agitated suddenly.

"No, you're here to find out what you can for that Jenny Reynolds," he said. "It won't do you any good she is going to be locked up before long."

"I need to talk to Anita," Tyler repeated.

"Really," Willie laughed. "You had better not get her all upset or you're the one who will be in trouble."

"Who said anything about causing trouble?" Tyler questioned not sure what Willie was going on about, but it was plain he did not want him here.

"You just worry about yourself and let us worry about how my sister is doing."

Anita appeared with a tray of lemonade and cookies. Pouring each of them a drink over ice cubes in glasses from the tray, she passed them out before taking a seat and offering them a cookie. Tyler had just eaten lunch and really didn't want a cookie, but he took one anyway.

"Tyler, I can't tell you how sorry I am that you were injured in the accident," she begins.

"Anita, you know Dad said you were not to talk about the accident with anyone," Willie said not giving her a chance to say anything else.

"I know, but Tyler was there," Anita looked confused for a moment before looking at Tyler as if she wasn't sure what else to say. "Willie is it okay if I ask Tyler how he is doing after the accident?"

"Anita …," Willie started to say.

"Well, really all you and dad can do is shadow me like hawks, like you don't think I can be left alone for a second. Then all you do is more or less tell me what I can and cannot say without your permission."

Tyler couldn't help but notice that Willie seemed upset, his sister had said that. He was again acting nervous about what she might say next. After several minutes of silence, Tyler said, "Actually, I am doing well, slowly getting my mobility back. I know my leg will never be back to what it was before and I may always have a limp, but I'm thankful to be able to get around."

"I'm glad," she replied. "Just sorry, that your basketball career is over. You were so much fun to watch in the National Championship games."

"Yeah, it was fun playing and I miss it," Tyler stated. "I'm still trying to get use to the idea I won't be playing the sport at that level ever again. Talking about me is not my reason for being here today, I wanted to visit and check on how you are doing."

"I've been better," Anita said. "I wake up each morning and hope the nightmare will go away. Unfortunately, it never does, I realize this is my life."

"These cookies are really good," he said taking another one. "I also wanted to say thank you for saving my life by getting me out of my car that night," Tyler said.

Anita smiled faded and she asked, "Who told you that?"

"No one told me, I just assumed it was you who got me out," Tyler replied as he watched the expressions on her face change. He could tell that something was not right, and he thought she was going to tell him something else. Unfortunately, he would never know if she would have said anything more because at that moment Ted Smith came charging out of the house just as tears began running down Anita's cheeks. "See I told you not to upset her! Willie started shouting. "Dad, I told him to not upset her!"

"No dad …," Anita began but was cut off by her father turning on Tyler. "What's the meaning of this?" Ted Smith was obviously angry that his daughter was in tears. "You come to my house without even calling to see me." "I came by your house to see Anita," Tyler said. "I don't recall you calling ahead when

You came by my grandfather's house the other day."

"He's been asking her things about the accident," Willie added.

Tyler had no difficulty in reading the body language of all three of the Smiths. Anita was nervous and had a tragic look on her face that made her look fragile. Willie had a look of pure glee on his face and threw back his head with an air of waiting to see what his father was going to do or say about Tyler questioning his sister.

"Actually, I was thanking her for getting me out of my car after the accident," Tyler replied. "I did not intend to cause her additional pain."

There was a strange expression that came over Anita's face and she said, "But I didn't."

"That's enough talk about the accident," Ted declared. "Anita, it's time you go in and take your medicine and I will deal with Tyler."

"I'm sorry …," Anita's voice was almost a whisper, but it was her eyes that were pleading with Tyler and for some unknown reason he felt she was asking him for help. Anita left the patio without another word, but it was at a very slow pace. She did not look like the girl who had met him at the door and insisted Willie show him to the patio. What was going on here?

"Willie, make sure she takes her pills," Ted said with a flash of anger when it looked as though Willie wasn't going to leave.

"He's been dating that Reynolds girl, he came here to get information that might help her," Willie insisted before leaving to follow his sister inside.

"I didn't know …," Tyler said.

"Save it, I think Willie knows what he is talking about," Ted said as he stares at Tyler.

"I was under the impression that Anita had to be the one to pull me from the car the night of the accident," he replied. "She said it wasn't her."

"Anita doesn't know what she is talking about," Ted declared. "She doesn't remember what happened that night."

"But she just …," Tyler responded.

"Forget what she said. She's under a lot of stress and doesn't know what she is saying," he said taking a step toward him. "Now, I am telling you to leave and not come around here again." The expression on his face held a degree of worry.

Tyler fixed Ted Smith with a skeptical look of his own. Then he walked back around the house and got in his truck. He looked up at a window on the second floor of the house and saw the curtain fall back in place. Someone was watching him leave and he couldn't help but wonder if it had been Anita or Willie. He didn't know what the pleading looks in her eyes had been about, but he was sure of one thing Anita had said she wasn't the one who pulled him from the car. The look in her eyes at that moment made him accept she was telling the truth.

Chapter Thirteen

The following week was one of the longest of Jenny's life. She went through her routine without giving much thought to what she was doing. As she starts her morning of checking her fields, she couldn't forget what had happened on Sunday when she went to church with Ruth. Thankfully, Tyler wasn't there with his grandparents, and she didn't have to see him. The Smiths were there, and she couldn't forget the penetrating gaze of the Smith family and how they had made her very uncomfortable, especially Mark's father. Anita had been at church for the first time in a long time but the one time that their eyes had met, Anita quickly looked away. Anita's brother, Willie, continued to display his feelings as he stared at her with bitterness and hatred in his eyes.

Then as she left church, she heard two of the older ladies in conversation. "Can you believe that girl is here again today? The poor Smith family have to be upset that she's still walking free and their son and brother are buried in the ground."

"She has a nerve to sit in God's house and act like she hasn't done anything wrong. You're right it must be hard on them. Ted has been through so much, first losing his wife at such a young age and now a son."

"That girl probably thinks if she goes to church, she won't have to go to jail for what she did," one of the ladies said.

"That's where she belongs for killing that poor boy. She hurt the McCall boy too, and he will never play basketball again. What a career he had."

She didn't listen to anymore, but as she had turned, she almost ran into Anita. It was plain from the look on Anita's face that she had also heard the conversation. Ted Smith had come up and grabbed his daughter by the arm giving Jenny one of his glaring stares and forcing Anita to go with him. The look of the raw pain in Anita's eyes just before she turned away still haunted her.

She was so focused on what had happened the day before, it took a moment to realize that there was something wrong with the jeep. It was soon obvious the pull to one side indicated she must have a flat. As she looked for a place to pull the jeep off the road, she couldn't help but notice it was in almost the same spot that Tyler had run her in the ditch only a few weeks before. Making sure she could be seen coming from both directions, she stopped the jeep, got out and moved to the back of the jeep to get out the jack and extra tire. Thankfully, her grandfather had taught her how to change her own tire if she should ever find herself in this position. It took her several minutes before she could loosen all the bolts so she could get the tire off once she jacked it up, and several more minutes to get the jack set up under the axle. She was almost ready to give up by the time she had the jeep jacked up high enough to get the tire off. The sound of a truck coming before she saw it had her looking up in time to see Tyler's truck. She was surprised when it pulled pass and stopped.

Looking up she saw Tyler get out of his truck and walk slowly toward her. She couldn't help but notice he was walking without the help of his crutches. He still had a slight limp, but he was moving well.

"Having tire problems, I see," Tyler said.

"Nothing I can't handle," she replied without looking up. Feeling his eyes resting on her she continued to concentrate on putting the bolts on before letting the jack back down.

"Pretty independent I see." "I'm used to taking care of myself," Jenny said. She couldn't help but add, "I would think I am the last person you would be offering help to."

"I can't just drive by and leave you here if you need help."

"As you can see, I don't need your help," Jenny replied rolling the flat tire out of the way where she could tighten the bolts. She still hadn't looked directly at Tyler. She didn't want him to see the dark circles under her eyes. She certainly didn't want him to know how much he had hurt her. All that was left of changing the tire was tightening the bolts then she could be on her way.

Tyler moved over and tightened the bolts before she could do it. Then he followed her to the back of the jeep and handed her the tire tool after she placed the jack back inside its compartment.

As she went to get the flat to put it in the jeep, Tyler said," I can drop your flat off at the station in town if you would like I'm on my way there now."

Jenny started to tell him not to worry about it, and then changed her mind. She would be able to pick up her tire without having to wait on it.

"Thanks, I am almost finished with checking traps in your grandfather's fields," Jenny said.

The next statement Tyler made was unexpected. "I talked to Anita last week. She said you use to be best friends."

"Use to be friends, seems to the operative word these days," she responded with a sad look on her face.

"They blame you for Mark's death."

Glazing up at him she couldn't hide the pain that was in her eyes. "Tell me something I don't know."

"What happened that night?"

Looking at him in surprise she said, "I thought you knew."

"Not all of it." He studied her face for a moment then looked away. "There are blanks, things I remember, sketches of things, but no, there is a lot I still don't remember. The doctor said I may not ever remember. It is my brain's way of coping."

"You want me to fill you in," she laughed at that.

"Yes."

"Why? Jenny asked. "What difference would it make?"

"Why not?" Tyler questioned softly. "Everyone knows you were the driver."

"I don't talk about it because it is too painful," Jenny insisted.

"I just want to know who pulled me out of my car that night." Tyler asked. "Just so you know, Anita said it wasn't her."

"So, you asked her." Jenny commented. "How did you get by her protectors?"

"Willie was there, and he didn't leave her side the whole time I was there," he said. "Ted was nowhere in sight when I arrived, but I think Willie sent him a message. He showed up and ordered me off his property and not to return."

"Why would he do that?" she asked.

"Seems he thinks we are dating, and I was trying to find out information to help you."

"I'm sure you corrected him on that thought," she said.

"I told him we weren't dating," Tyler said. "I don't think he was bothered by that. I think it was more about what I was there asking his daughter."

"Even while we were friends her father would watch her like a hawk. Overprotective is not even the word for it," Jenny said. "It is a wonder she even got the chance to attend the party that night. Mark is a totally different story. He could do whatever he wanted. I guess it had something to do with her being the only girl."

"What are they afraid of? Tyler asked. "Are they afraid she might harm herself?"

"How did she seem?"

"She seemed okay at first. She is certainly and understandably sad if you ask me," he replied. "She did invite me to stay when Willie more or less was trying to make me go."

"She was so vibrant before the accident," Jenny said sadly. "I done even want to think about the pain losing her twin brother must have caused her. I wish I could help her." Tears were at the surface again, but she would not let Tyler see her cry.

"So, will you fill me in on what happened that night, Jenny?"

"Why, so you can use it against me when we go to court?" Jenny declared. "No! Don't think so." "Is that what you think?" Tyler demanded as he put out his hand and caught her shoulder when she went to walk away. "Look Jenny, I think Anita knows more than she is saying, but I get the feeling her father and Willie are controlling her in some way. Do you think it is possible she needs help?"

"Ted Smith has always been controlling where Anita is concerned. If you think she needs help, her grandmother would move heaven and earth if she thought she needed to get in to see her. Your grandmother will know how to get in touch with her. What happened that night is better left buried," she answered. "It doesn't change a thing. Mark is dead, your career is ruined, and my best friend may never be the same."

She rolled the tire over to the back of Tyler's truck. She lifted it into the back before turning around to go back to her jeep.

"Thank you for your help. Please tell Henry I will be by later to pick it up and pay him." Jenny said.

Walking over to her jeep she got in and fastened her seat belt before cranking the engine and driving off. She was glad she didn't have to do anything more demanding than pulling up to the traps and checking for boll weevils. At least she knew Tyler would still speak to her even if all he wanted to know was what happened that night. *What he would never understand, she couldn't tell him or anyone about what really happened the night of the accident. It was all water under the bridge now anyway, and nothing would change the outcome or make it better.*

Chapter Fourteen

Jenny pulled into the only gas station in town that fixed flats later that day. She had finished scouting and gone home to finish her report and sent it in. Running into town, to pick up her tire before she had another flat and got stranded somewhere, was the last thing on her agenda for the day. She got out of her jeep and walked over to Henry, a tall black boy was working on a tire. He looked up and smiled at her.

"Your tire is ready," he said. Whipping sweat from his brow with a large rag he returned it to his back pocket.

"Can I get you to put the tire back on my jeep for me?" she asked. "I don't like driving on the spare."

"Sure, have a coke and it won't take but a few more minutes for me to change the tire for you. I just need to finish this tire I am working on first."

Jenny went inside and got a cold coke from a large bucket of iced drinks. She had just walked back outside when a truck with loud pipes came roaring down the street. Several guys were hanging out the window yelling as they passed by. The driver jammed on his brakes and swung in behind Jenny's jeep almost hitting it. Willie left the engine running and hopped out.

"Well, well, what do we have here?" Willie jeered as he moved in front of Jenny.

"Trouble by the looks of it," Steve Miller, Willie's best friend laughed as he hopped out of the back of the truck and came to join in the fun.

"What do you want Willie?" Jenny asked as she tried to move away from him.

"Not so fast! Willie declared. "Sheriff came by to visit us the other day and my dad was pretty mad at you lying about us like you did. What? Are you trying to do build up sympathy before you get locked away thinking they might not send you to jail?" He laughed. "Don't worry, my dad is making sure you pay for what you did. You're going down and that crazy daddy of yours better think twice before he puts his hands on my old man again."

"I don't want any trouble, Willie, so leave me alone." Jenny replied, trying to stay calm. The other guys were now out of the truck, and they had surrounded her. She didn't think they would harm her there in the middle of the town, but the look in Willie's eyes was frightening. She had never experienced the look of pure hate before that he kept directing at her and she didn't know what to do about it.

"You need to leave me alone, there are witnesses here and I will report you again. This time you might not be so lucky with erasing evidence." Jenny said.

"You do know you're going to pay," Willie whispered as he got in her face. "It's only a matter of the right place and the right time. I'll be there when you least expect it."

"Are you threatening me?" Jenny asked moving as far away from him as she could. "Because if you are …"

"By the time I'm finished with you, you'll wish you were the one who died," he sneered. "That's a promise!"

"What's the problem here?" Tyler McCall demanded as he crossed the pavement to the group of guys surrounding Jenny. He looked angry as he approached the group.

"You again! You need to mind your own business!" Willie shouted.

"I'm making it my business," Tyler replied.

"She crippled you in the wreck," Willie remarked. "Why do you want to defend her?"

"Just say, I don't like to see anyone being harassed." Tyler answered.

"She deserves everything she's going to get," Willie sneered again. "You had better mind your own business or you might get some of the same."

"You are threatening her!" Tyler said. "If you know what's good for you go home and leave her alone!"

"Come on, Willie," Steve said catching him by the arm. "Here come the cops."

"Don't worry, I'll see you at a time and place of my choosing," he announced looking at Jenny as he backed away jumping into his truck, roaring off down the street away from the approaching police cruiser.

"Problem?" Officer Johnson asked as he got out of the police car looking after the truck that had just pulled out. "Henry said he thought there might be trouble."

"Willie was just mouthing off," Jenny answered. "He was threatening her," Tyler added. "Those weren't idol words. He is an angry young man who wants revenge."

"Then I guess the two of you have something in common," Jenny couldn't help adding.

"I am nothing like Willie," Tyler said. It was obvious he did not like Jenny comparing him to Willie.

"Just saying."

"Do we need to make a report?" Officer Johnson asked, drawing their attention back to him.

"No, I don't want to cause more trouble for his family."

"He was promising to hurt you!" Tyler declared not believing she was taking Willies' threats so lightly.

"Look Tyler, I've known Willie a long time and he is just mouthing off trying to scare me and look big in front of his friends," she said. Hopefully that was all he meant.

"He sounds pretty serious to me."

"We can write up a report about this call Jenny," the officer offered. "Unless you want to press charges since no harm was done that is about all we can do for now. You could get a restraining order so he can't come near you, and we can arrest him if he does."

Jenny shook her head. "I just want to forget it," she finally said after being silent for several seconds.

"Surely there is something more that can be done," Tyler declared. "He just told her he plans for her to pay for his brother's death." "The family is suing for a lot of money and property, so that might be what he meant by paying," Officer Johnson suggested. "I think he means more," Tyler insisted again.

"I can't do anything unless you press charges. It's your call Jenny," the officer waited for her to decide.

"I can't do that."

"Then I think you should be careful not to be caught out alone. You need to watch for and report any other incidents." Officer Johnson added, "I will talk to his father again, but I know the family is still pretty torn up about Mark's death."

Henry came for the jeep to change the tire.

Officer Johnson went back to his patrol car and got in. He sat there filling out his report and when he got out again, he told Jenny that he would follow up with a visit to see Willie and his father before the day was out.

"Thank you, Officer Johnson. I do appreciate your quick response today."

"You really need to keep your safety in mind and be careful."

Tyler continued to stand there beside Jenny even after the officer pulled away. "You're not to go out and scout fields again by yourself," he declared. "It's not safe especially now with Willie threatening you."

"I don't need a babysitter," Jenny responded, not liking Tyler bossing her. "Be reasonable about this." Henry waved at Jenny to let her know her tire was back on, and she was ready to go. She went inside to pay for the repairs and her drink. When she went outside and got into the jeep, Tyler walked up to her side and put his hand on her door.

"I mean it, Jenny. You're not to go out into those fields again by yourself. Willie is angry and there is no telling what he might do. You're going to listen to me, right?"

"Look, I have to scout my fields," Jenny said.

"Come by and get me, I'll ride with you."

"No!"

"What do you mean, no?" Tyler was getting frustrated with her stubbornness. "If you want to continue to scout our fields you will."

"Are you going to get me fired?"

"If I have to," Tyler said with a frustrated look on his face.

"You're really serious about this?" Jenny questioned although she could already see he was. "Why do you even care?"

Tyler looked at her for a moment, not sure why he was being so determined to see she was safe. "I don't want to see you harmed, Jenny."

"I'll talk to my dad and see if I can find someone who can ride with me," she finally said pulling away not giving Tyler a chance to say anything else. Did he think she would ask him to ride with her again? No way was that going to happen. She just needed to keep in mind he didn't want anything to do with her. Besides, why was he acting like he cared?

Chapter Fifteen

The following day Tyler had asked his grandmother to go with him to see Anita's grandmother. Louise Mayfield was a lovely gray-headed woman in her early sixties, who greeted them at the front steps of her home and asked them to join her on her front porch. She had been working in her flower beds and removed her gloves to shake Tyler's hand.

"Hello Tyler," Louise said. "It is good to see you up and about. You don't know me, but I've been following you for a while with the Razorback basketball team. I was sad that your accident interrupted you're playing."

"Thanks. I'm glad you have time to see us, Mrs. Mayfield," Tyler replied.

"I understand from what your grandmother said on the phone you're concerned for my granddaughter," Louise said. "For that I want to say thank you."

"I think she needs help to escape her father and Willie's constant hovering over her," Tyler said. "I was only at their place for a short time, but I got the feeling that she isn't allowed to have a conversation that someone isn't listening in on. It was the pleading look in her eyes that said please help me that has me here today," he added.

"The controlling part sounds like her father," Louise agreed. "I've not been allowed to see Anita for some time now. After my daughter

Susan died, Ted started making it harder and harder for me to see the kids. Then after Mark's death, it's been almost impossible. The last time I visited I didn't even get to see her, just Willie and he is just like his dad."

"I'm sorry, Louise," Alma said. "I didn't realize that you didn't get to see your grandkids."

"It's been hard. Their father has all the say in the matter, but I'm just a grandparent," Louise said sadly. "Now, you've given me a reason to get out there. If he doesn't let me see her, I am going to file something in court if I have to."

"Ted told me not to return so I can't go back out there, but do you know any of Anita's friends besides Jenny Reynolds that might get in to see her. Maybe we could set up visitors that might be able to get messages in and out, so we can know if she needs our help. I would really like to know she's okay."

"Christy Rivers is one of Anita's friends I think we can count on to help us," Louise said. "I'm pretty sure she knows some more girls that could help if we need them. Now, if you will excuse me, I'm going to change clothes and go see Anita. I'm not going to call Ted, just show up. Think I will pack a bag and stay a few days and see what he says about that. I'll demand to see her, and I know if I threaten Ted with taking him to court, he'll let me at least see her. I'll also call my friend Carrie, that's Christy's grandmother. She'll help me get Christy involved. As soon as I see Anita, I'll let you know what's going on."

"Thanks, Mrs. Mayfield," Tyler said. "I feel time is of the essence."

"No Tyler, I am the one who thanks you for having the courage to speak up and do something when you feel there's something wrong. Not everyone will do that," Louise said as if she had firsthand experience of what she was saying.

"Please keep us informed, Louise," Alma said hugging her friend before going to Tyler's truck.

Tyler got in and closed the door, buckling his seat belt before cranking the engine. As he looked over at his grandmother their eyes meet and his grandmother smiled at him before saying, "You know, Louise is right about so many people seeing something wrong and turn away without doing anything about it. I'm proud of you for following through."

"I just hope someone can get in there and help her."

"Louise is a grandmother that loves her granddaughter, and I know she'll not rest till she knows Anita's all right."

"Did I tell you that Anita said she didn't pull me from the car that night?" Tyler asked as he backed up and put the truck in drive to head home.

"No, you didn't tell me that," Alma said. "That means it had to be Jenny who got you out. How do you feel about that?"

"Ashamed of my behavior," Tyler replied. "Especially, after the things I said to her when I found out who she was."

"Jenny has had to face a lot the last few years. Her mother left her with her grandparents while Dave was deployed. Then both grandparents got sick and died within weeks of each other. Her father came home hurt and suffering from PTSD. Add to all of that, after the accident Ruth took her in when she had nowhere else to go. Jenny has been on her own for a large part of her teen years."

"Then I say the things I did to her. That makes it even worse," Tyler said with a sad look on his face.

"I know you were disappointed when your grandfather and I didn't tell you who she was. We felt if you got to know her you would give her a chance. People make mistakes, that's a part of life. Most are lucky enough not to have such a terrible life changing event happen to them. One they have to live with for the rest of their life."

"I'm trying to find out what's going on with Anita because I have a feeling what's happening with her has something to do with the accident," Tyler stated. "I keep getting snipes of things from that night. They don't make sense. I awoke twice, and its always Jenny's voice I hear calling for someone to help her."

"Maybe Louise will be able to find out what is going on with her."

"I guess we just need to go home and wait to hear from her then," Tyler said.

Chapter Sixteen

J enny knew Tyler would be really upset with her if he knew she was scouting her fields by herself again today. She had tried to call her dad, but he had not called her back, so she had got up early and headed out. Jenny walked into the tall cotton stalks after taking her recording tools and two sticks with a dark rectangle cloth attaching them together. She laid the two sticks down between two rows where the rectangle cloth would catch any bugs or worms that fell off the cotton plants. Catching the cotton stalks mid-way up on each row, she gives them a good shake. A moment later, she counts the number of bugs and worms that lay on the dark cloth before recording them. She smiled when she counted a ladybug which was considered a good bug.

She was about to stand up when something caused her to pause for a moment. *Was that voices?* The cotton was high enough that she couldn't see her jeep, but she could hear someone near it. A moment later she recognized Willie's voice saying,

"She's around here someplace. Get over there, be quite and we'll surprise her when she comes back."

"Come on, Willie let's get out of here before someone sees us and we get in trouble," Steve said.

"Be quiet," Willie said again. "I've been watching her. She will be back shortly."   Jenny kept her head down and eased away from the voices. Slowly she moved down the middle of the row. Stopping to listen, she paused for just a moment, but as she started to take another step, she saw two big black snakes in the middle of the row. Frozen in place her heart jumped into her throat. One of the snakes was looking directly at her. It seemed to move toward her and was only inches from her foot when she closed her eyes and stayed frozen in place.

"Jesus, please help me…Jesus, Jesus, Jesus, there is a name I will remember… Jesus, Jesus, Jesus, there is a name I will proclaim… Jesus, Jesus, Jesus help me in this moment," Jenny whispered over and over again. The fear she first felt left her as she continued saying the name of Jesus. She was not sure how long she repeated the phrases, but when she finally opened her eyes and looked down at her feet, the snakes were gone. Taking out her phone with shaking hands she quickly sent a text message to Thomas and her dad. She told them where she was hiding in the cotton patch across the road from the turn off to the McCall's farm, that Willie was waiting for her and she needed help fast.

She wasn't sure how much time passed before hearing a rustling in the stalks near where she was hiding. She realized that Willie or one of the other guys were tired of waiting and came into the cotton patch to find her. They were moving closer to her. *Lord, please protect me, don't let them find me.*

"Snakes! Watch out, there are snakes in here! Run!" Willie's high-pitched scream came from close by and she could hear him running back the way he came.

From the frantic rustling not far away, she knew the other boys were hard on his heels, some laughing as they went. "Man let's get out of here," one of them said.

Moments later, she heard the pipes on Willie's truck roar before he took off across a part of the field where there was no cotton planted.

Willie thought it was a quick path leading to the main road. Jenny knew he was about to come to a stop and couldn't help the smile that appeared on her face. She too had learned the hard way why no cotton was planted there. All she had to do was stay put until help arrived. Surely someone would be there before long. *Thank You, Lord, for your protection. Please let help get here soon.* A few minutes later she heard a siren in the distance coming closer and closer. She slowly made her way out of the cotton field still holding on to her report and the sticks with the cloth attached to them. She recognized the sheriff's SUV pulling in, but it was her dad's truck pulling in behind her jeep that made her feel safe. She could see the fear on her dad's face until he saw her coming out of the cotton patch.

"Did they hurt you?" he asked as he rushed over to her, she and put his arms around her.

"No, I am okay," Jenny said but there were tears in her voice as she clung to him. "They scared me, Dad. Then there were snakes in the cotton patch that scared me too. They ran Willie and the other boys out before they got to me. Willie's truck is now stuck, he was trying to take a short cut to the main road just before you got here. That field is deceiving it has soft spots that you can quickly sink into." Jenny could see the sheriff already had the boys lined up outside the vehicle.

"Bob was at the farm when I got your text. He radioed ahead but there was no one as close as we were. He said he would call for backup on the way."

Sirens sounded in the distance as another deputy's car pulled up near the sheriff's SUV. Jenny heard the Sheriff say, "Watch these guys and I will be back in a moment."

Bob Warren came toward them. Looking over at her jeep all the tires were slashed, and the CB radio cord had been cut. "Jenny, are you hurt?"

"No, just scared," she said. "But yes sir, to pressing charges this time."

"Did you see them do this?" Bob asked.

"I heard them over by the jeep, but I didn't see them cut my tires or anything. I hid in the cotton field when I heard them. Although I didn't see them do it, I know they did." Jenny said wondering if it would be like last time they would get off because they could deny it. One against five.

"Stay away from the jeep and we will get the footprints that I am sure will match most of the shoes in Willie's truck." Bob told them.

"Are you going to arrest them?" Dave asked.

"Yes, I am," Bob said. "They might even get to spend a little time in the slammer before I will let them bond out. Might do some of them good, wake up a few parents if nothing else."

"Jenny, you can go with your dad, and he'll take you by the city police department. You can fill out the statement for the paperwork there and you can sign it. I'll be along in a little bit and will take the report in with me. You don't need to go to Hamburg," Bob told her. "Leave the jeep as it is, and I'll have it towed after the evidence is collected."

The sheriff walked back to all five boys with handcuffs standing beside Willies truck. He had two of the boys put in his car. Two in another patrol car and Willie were placed alone in the last one that had just pulled up. Jenny heard him tell the other officers, "Make sure the boys are kept separate from Willie once you get them to the jail. Put Willie in the integration room first and let him sit until I get there."

"Come on Jenny, we'll go get this done," her dad said leading her over to his truck. "Getting this report written up while it is still fresh is the most important thing you need to do right now. We'll come back and finish your fields latter."

"We need to tell the McCall's what is going on," she said as her father backed up to leave. As she placed a hand on the cross of the necklace she wore, she bowed her head in a prayer of thanksgiving. *Jesus, I want to thank You for being there beside me today. I felt Your present and I know it was You who used those snakes as a weapon to protect me. You've been here for me from the start, Lord and I know that I am Yours and that You are mine. You are my friend, and I know You love me. I will not worry about tomorrow, I don't know what it holds, but I know who holds tomorrow. I want You to know I love You and I will forever be thankful that You will always be here for me.*

Chapter Seventeen

Tyler was almost to Wilmot when he had to pull his truck over to let a police car with its blue lights flashing go by. Before he could pull back onto the roadway, he had to wait for a state trooper who was also moving at a high rate of speed.

"Wonder where they're going in such a hurry?" Alma asked, reaching for her phone to call her husband. Her cell phone dinged indicating an incoming text before she could dial.

As she read it, she said, "Oh, no, we must get to the farm. Jenny's in some kind of trouble at the ten acres field. Your grandfather says there are cops at the field across from the turnoff into our place."

"Is Jenny hurt? Did he say if she is okay?" Tyler exclaimed his heart rate accelerating as he sped up. *Lord, please let Jenny be all right.*

"No, but something is going on," Alma said. She called her husband and when he answered she said, "Thomas is Jenny okay? You're sure? Law is there. Tyler and I will be there shortly." She hung up and bowed her head as in prayer, praying for Jenny because she didn't know what was happening or if she was hurt.

Tyler didn't want to interrupt her, but he was anxious to know what was going on. He slowed down as he went through town and over the railroad tracks. He picked up speed again once out of the city limits. It seemed like forever before he could see flashing lights ahead.

He turned into their road and pulled past his grandfather's vehicle, so he wasn't blocking anyone. Getting out of his truck, he hurried over beside his grandfather, his grandmother was right behind him.

"What's going on?" Tyler asked. "Is Jenny all right."

"I think so. She was talking to the sheriff a few minutes ago and she looked okay at the time. Her dad's over there too. I saw his truck pulled in behind the sheriffs. I'm sure it has something to do with those boys stuck over there in the field."

Tyler looked at where his grandfather pointed. He saw five boys in handcuffs being put into police cars. He wasn't surprised that Willie was one of them and he was mouthing off as he was being put into a car by himself. Whatever he was shouting no one seemed to be listening.

He saw Jenny's dad put her into his truck and finally let out the breath he had been holding, relieved just knowing she wasn't hurt. Dave went around and got in his truck backing up and turning around to leave. He pulled across the road and stopped beside them.

"We are on our way to City Hall to file charges against the boys just arrested. Jenny's okay but knew you would want to know. I'll bring her back out to finish her fields once we complete the paperwork," Dave said.

"Thanks for letting us know she's okay," Thomas said. "Don't worry about the fields. We do want to hear the whole story so if you could stop back by later today, that would be great." Tyler could see Jenny in the passenger seat, but she was looking out the window on the other side. He wanted to go around and confront her because he was certain she had gone out to scout the cotton fields by herself. When they came by later, he would talk to her in front of the others and make sure they were aware of the other things Willie had been up to. He was sure both his grandfather and her dad would see someone rode with her when she scouted her fields from now on.

"Better yet, why don't you and Jenny join us for dinner around 6 o'clock?" Alma said.

"That should be okay, we can discuss what happened then," Dave said. "Jenny still has fields to finish and has to get her report in." He backed out into the road and headed back toward town.

****

Jenny was quiet as they drove away from the McCall's road. She wasn't looking forward to telling the story about what had happened that morning. She realized now it was time Willie faced up to the things he'd been doing. He was Mark and Anita's brother and if something wasn't done to cause him to see his bullying was wrong then he was only going to continue until something more serious happened. Most of the guys with him today were not troublemakers, but they were letting Willie influence them to do something they normally wouldn't have done.

"How do you feel about us eating dinner at the McCall's home tonight?" her dad asked as they drove away.

"It's fine dad, I think Tyler is going to stress again how it isn't safe for me to be scouting by myself," Jenny said. "After today, I would have to agree. I'm not sure what Willie would have done if he'd found me in the field. I think he was just trying to scare me, but when I didn't come back, they messed up my jeep. On top of that, I could have gotten snake bit, but the same snakes that could have bitten me ran Willie from the field. I must believe that wasn't an accident. Dad, I believe God protected me today. I guess you might not think I am making much sense, but when I was so scared and started to pray, I felt Him. I know He saved me today."

Dave Reynolds pulled into a parking space at the City Hall and cut the engine. He reached over and took his daughter hand and said, "You may be right. I know He saved me more than once while I served our country. I believe I'm here today because He saved me that day in the desert. I still don't know why I paused to move into position but if I had not stopped when I did, I would have been in the middle of the firepower instead of on the edge of it. I was wounded, my career was over, but I was still alive. I'll forever thank God for giving me a chance to do something more and to be here for you now."

"I know now what Grandma use to talk about when she said when He brings someone to mind, she always says a prayer for them. She told me she said a lot of prayers while you were over there. Today when the two snakes were in the row with me, and one was just inches away, Dad, I closed my eyes and started saying Jesus over and over with some words from a song that came to mind. I was really scared at first, but I felt His presence. It was like a sense of peace came over me and I was no longer afraid. When I again opened my eyes, the snakes were gone, and I was able to send the message for help. I'm not sure how much time passed before I heard Willie and the other boys coming into the field. Then suddenly, Willie's screaming snakes and is running out of the field with the others following right behind him."

"Let's go get this over with," Dave said. "We can talk more about this later."

Giving her statement wasn't as bad as Jenny thought. A deputy took her to a room and let her tell what had happened. She was glad they let her dad stay with her. She was asked only a few questions afterward. Then the statement was typed up. She read over it before signing. In less than forty-five minutes they were on their way out of the office. As they walked out the door the sheriff was pulling in.

Jenny went to her father's truck, but her father waited on Bob to walk to the door.

"Here to pick up the statement and get over to the jail and get some interviews," Bob said. "I'm thankful we were there as quick as we were, I would have hated for anything to happen to Jenny. I don't want her to scout any more by herself. Either someone needs to ride with her, or someone else needs to do her job."

"I agree," Dave said.

"I'll call you later," Bob said and went inside for Jenny's statement.

"Thanks, Dad," Jenny said as her father got in the truck. "I'm glad you're here."

"Me too," he said. "You want to get those fields finished?" He cranked the engine before putting the truck in reverse and backing out of the parking space. He then drove back the way they had come.

Chapter Eighteen

Tyler was sitting on the porch with his grandfather talking about the eventful day. They saw Louise's car coming down the driveway. After getting out of the car Louise moved around her car to the passenger's side. She opened the door and helped her granddaughter Anita out. They walked up the sidewalk with Louise keeping an arm around Anita.

"Thomas, I hope you don't mind us dropping by like this, but we need your help," Louise said as she reached the steps.

"You know I'll do anything I can," Thomas said. "Come on in. Alma's inside preparing dinner. I know she'll be glad to see you. Anita, it is good to see you."

Anita's eyes were downcast, and she appeared to be a little dazed, not smiling or acting like she had been spoken to. Tyler thought she was not at all like she had been the day he had gone to talk to her. He watched with a concerned look on his face as her grandmother guided her into the house.

"I need to sit down," Anita said in almost a whisper.

"Here dear, sit here on the sofa," her grandmother urges her.

Alma walks into the room from the kitchen and hurries over to assist getting Anita to sit down. There was a worried look on her face as she saw the shape Anita was in. Her face was very pale, and her eyes were dilated indicating she had been given or taken some type of drug. Is she okay?"

"I found her like this when I got to the house and no one else was home," Louise said.

"Has she been drugged?" Alma asked.

"I'm pretty sure Ted gave her something before he left the house to make her sleep," Louise said. "I am almost certain that is what he's been doing to control her."

"How did you get her out of the house?" Alma asked.

"No one was home when I got there," Louise said.

"Your grandson Willie was arrested this afternoon. He and some of his friends were in our fields trying to scare Jenny and did something to her jeep. The sheriff arrested the whole bunch of them, and I am sure Ted is over at the County Jail trying to get Willie out," Thomas told her.

"Really?" She laughed. "I will say God does work in mysteries ways. I was praying on the way I'd be able to see my granddaughter. Then there was no one home when I got there. The front door was locked, but I went around to the patio doors. They were unlocked. I went in and found Anita upstairs in her room asleep. I was finally able to wake her up, get her dressed, downstairs, and into my car. I decided to pack some clothes for her before I left. Now, I'm almost afraid to go back to my house in case Ted shows up and tries to take Anita back home."

"What can we do to help?" Alma asked. "Can we stay here a few days?" Louise asked. "Ted won't think to look for us here. "If you think that'll help Anita then I will say yes," Alma replied looking over at Thomas and Tyler who had followed them inside. "We have plenty of room. We may want to let Bob Warren know she's here, because

I think Ted will file a missing person report as soon as he realizes she is missing."

"That's fine with me. I assume we don't have to say where we are. I'll tell you now, Anita's not going back to that house until I'm convinced, she's okay," Louise said.

"Let's get Anita upstairs and into bed. She looks like she needs to sleep off whatever Ted gave her," Alma said. "Thomas put Louise's car in our garage. That way no one will know they're here."

Louise had tears in her eyes and gave Alma a hug. "May God bless you for this," Louise said. Turning she touched Tyler on the arm. "Thank you for coming and telling me about Anita. Would you bring the suitcases from the back seat?"

Alma helped Louise get Anita upstairs and into bed. Then Alma went downstairs and fixed Louise a plate of food. Louise wanted to stay upstairs with Anita in case she woke up and wouldn't know where she was. Tyler had taken the suitcases up to their room.

Tyler was helping set the table for dinner when he heard his grandfather say Jenny and her dad had arrived. He had been afraid for her when he heard she was in trouble today. Before she left tonight, he was determined to make sure she would not be scouting again by herself. He would ride with her if he had to. He was reminded of the day she had taken him scouting with her for the first time. A lot has happened since then.

Hearing his grandfather greeting them, he walked into the hallway to say hello.

Jenny hardly acknowledges him at all, and only said a few words as he approached. She let her father do most of the talking. He was glad when his grandmother came in and said dinner was ready.

Alma had made fried chicken and potato salad with several different vegetables fresh from the garden, they joined hands and bowed their heads for Thomas to say the blessing over the food.

"Lord, we thank you for this food and for those who share this meal with us. Bless us and keep us as we move forward. Amen."

Tyler held Jenny's hand during the short blessing and was slow to release it.

The conversation flowed around stories about how life on the farm had changed over the last few years. Some of the stories were funny and it was good to hear laughter. Jenny watched her dad and was glad he seemed to be enjoying the meal and the conversation until they finished with dessert and were sitting around the table.

"I've got a confession to make," Jenny told them, and everyone stopped talking and turned to hear what she had to say. "I made a mistake going out by myself today. I knew Willie was upset and was going to do something by what he said to me yesterday in town. Tyler warned me not to scout by myself. I called you, dad, before leaving this morning, but when you didn't answer I decided to go it alone. I would like to finish scouting if you will let me. If you allow me to do so, someone will need to ride with me."

"We don't have a problem with that, Jenny," Thomas said. "We agreed you can no longer scout by yourself before you got here. Tyler has agreed to ride with you for the rest of the week. I also have a jeep that you can use until yours is fixed. Since it happened on my property, I am going to pay to fix yours, and I will file a claim for the boys who did the damage to pay me back. I have already talked to Bob about this, and he thinks that it would be a good thing to do.

After they ate, Jenny helped wash dishes and put them away. Thomas had given her the keys to a jeep she could use until she had her own back. The adults were sitting out on the front porch talking, while Jenny was left alone with Tyler. She knew Tyler was glad her dad had agreed to ride on days that it wasn't convenient for him to help.

"Would you like to get some fresh air and join me on the back porch?" Tyler asked when the last of the dishes were put away.

"Yes, I would like that." Jenny followed him from the kitchen out onto the back porch. They stood by the deck railing looking out at the sun setting in the western sky. "It is so beautiful this time of the day. Just look at all the colors of that sunset," Jenny said loving this time of day and wishing she could paint a picture of the changing colors as the sun slowly disappeared. The night slowly surrounded them with the sounds of crickets and the crocking of frogs.

Tyler led the way over to the porch swing and let Jenny sit down before lowering himself slowly onto the other side of the swing. He let his leg stay straight and the swing was barely moving back and forth.

"I'm sorry, Tyler, that I didn't listen to your advice about scouting alone," Jenny said. "I keep thinking if someone else had been with me today, there is a good chance that the group of boys may not be in the trouble they are in. They may not have gotten arrested today. "You're feeling sorry for Willie and his friends?" Tyler asked. "They chose to do something that they knew was wrong, but they did it anyway. Don't feel sorry for them." "Not sorry, but disappointed. Would you believe most of those guys were my friends a year ago," Jenny said. "They were my classmates, now I guess you could say we seem to be enemies."

"I feel I need to apologize for the way I've treated you," Tyler replied. "It certainly wasn't very Christian of me to treat you so badly."

"I'm not sure I would have treated you any differently if I had been in your shoes," Jenny said as regret settled over her tightening her chest. She knew her feelings for Tyler had at one time been nothing more than a crush of a younger girl for an older guy. Now, the more she got to know him the more she cared about him. A lump formed in her throat when she considered she was probably the last person he was likely to develop any feelings for.

"I keep thinking all of us could have died that night," Tyler said quietly.

"Your right, we could have died," Jenny commented. "God still has plans for our lives, I'm just not sure what His plans for mine are right now."

"I don't have any idea about mine either," Tyler agreed.

"I know my life is held in limbo right now, depending on what happens in court in a few days. One thing I do know, God has control of the situation, and I will trust Him with the outcome. He let me live the night of the accident, and He saved me in that cotton patch today, from snakes, and from whatever Willie was going to do. The same snakes that held me frozen and praying to Jesus were the same ones that run Willie out of that field. I'll never believe that happened by accident. I know for a fact that as soon as I started praying for His help the peace and comfort, I felt could only have come from Him."

"I'm glad you are okay, Jenny. I know I've been mad at you about what happened to me. When I first arrived, I was set on seeing you pay for my injuries and the end of my career. Not knowing who you were at first, it gave me a chance to get to know you. I liked you right from the start. Then I was angry all over again, when I found out who you were because I thought you were playing me for a fool."

"I wasn't..." Jenny began.

"No, let me finish," Tyler said. "All my life I have been raised in a Christian family. I had this idea that I was living the Christian life and doing and being what Christ wanted me to be. Then one night my life got wrecked. I will have to say I started questioning God. Why did this happen to me? What did I do to deserve this? It's taken some time, but I realized God knows what He's doing. And who am I to question Him? I want you to know I no longer want to see you punished for what happened to me. I do want to know the truth of what happened that night. Will you tell me?"

"Tyler, I can't undo what happened that night. If I could Mark would be here, and we wouldn't be having this conversation. You wouldn't know me, and you would be on some basketball court practicing for the next big game."

"But we are here," Tyler whispered as he looked into Jenny's eyes at the sadness she couldn't hide. "Tell me about that night."

"I can't," she responded, and Tyler noticed tears running down her face.

"What are you hiding?" Tyler asked.

"I'm not hiding anything," she replied wanting to share with him, but she felt the secrets of that night were better left in the dark.

"I don't know what it is, but I know that there's more to the story than what you're telling. I wish I could remember. It's like it is right there on the edge of my memory but the more I try to remember the more distant it becomes.

"Just let it go, Tyler, remembering will not change anything," Jenny said as she stood up. "I think I am going to head on home. I'll pick you up around seven in the morning." She waved as she left him sitting in the swing.

Chapter Nineteen

Tyler was waiting on the front porch when Jenny pulled up. He had a small cooler he placed behind his seat before getting in. Jenny couldn't help but remember the first time he rode with her to scout cotton. He was now able to walk without his crutches and the smile he gave her disarmed her as he got in beside her.

"Good morning, Jenny," he said as he fastened his seatbelt.

"Hey Tyler, it is going to be a hot one today. The radio said temperature would be near 100 and the heat index will be over 105. Good thing it shouldn't take too long to get the scouting done today. We have the day off tomorrow for the 4th of July. Are you going to any of the celebrations in Hamburg?"

"Granddad said we were going to the program and the firework show," Tyler said. "What about you?"

"My dad and I are going over for the program. I like the firework show, but not sure if my dad will want to stay for it."

They pulled into the first field and Jenny got to work. The temperature was already starting to climb, and she knew they would be hot in the jeep without a top as they traveled around to the different fields. She parked in the shade when she could, but when it wasn't possible Tyler tried to find a bit of some kind of shade each time they stopped. It took the whole morning to get to all the fields. At their last stop when Jenny had finished her scouting and paperwork, she walked over and turned on a water hydrant and put her head under it to cool off. The water was cold, and it wasn't long before Tyler came over and joined her.

"That feels really good," he said as he splashed water on his face and put his head under the water.

"This is the best part after finishing work," Jenny laughed. "It'll make the ride back much more enjoyable. You ready to go home or do you want to take a trip out to our picnic spot?" Jenny asked.

"I've got to get back today," Tyler replied. "I didn't say anything last night, but Anita's at our house. Louise brought her over last night before you came for supper."

"Really?" Jenny was surprised. What would Anita be doing at the McCall's place? She wondered. She couldn't believe she'd been so near Anita and hadn't even known it.

"It seems her grandmother has stepped in and taken her from Ted because she thinks she needs rescuing." He looked over at Jenny like he was waiting for a reaction from her.

"I can't see Mr. Smith letting her do that without a fight," Jenny said.

"He wasn't there. He was over getting Willie out of jail." Tyler said with a smile on his face. `

"So, he doesn't know where Anita is? Jenny asked. "Correct," Tyler agreed. "I have a feeling he isn't going to be too pleased when he finds out."

"I'm pretty sure that's an understatement. How does she seem?"

"Last night she was really out of it. We think her dad had given her something to make her sleep. Of course, she wasn't up when I left this morning."

"Go easy on her, will you," Jenny said as she put the jeep in gear to take Tyler home. "She has been through a lot."

"I'm sure her grandmother is not going to let anyone upset her, so stop worrying about her."

"She was my best friend for a long time," Jenny said. She wanted to ask Tyler some more questions, but she wasn't sure what he would think so she kept them to herself. It didn't take long to drive Tyler back to his grandparent's place.

"See you Thursday," Tyler said. He got out as soon as she came to a stop. He gave her a wave, but he didn't look back. Jenny wasn't sure what she expected on this first day, but she hadn't expected it to end exactly like this. Backing up she headed toward Miss Ruth's place to file her report. Then she would be free until Thursday. A day off was just what she needed.

****

Jenny had just finished sending in her report and heard the doorbell ring. She went into the living room just as Miss Ruth answered the door. She heard her name mentioned so she walked over to the door and saw her father standing there. The serious look on his face let her know that something was wrong, or he wouldn't be there, especially when they were going to Hamburg the next day for the program.

"Dad, what's wrong?" she asked before he could say anything.

Ruth stood back and motioned for him to come in. He walked through the door and went into the living room and stood by one of the recliners. He waited for Ruth and Jenny to have a seat before he spoke. "Jenny, I heard from the new attorney this morning. I thought you needed to know that Ted Smith has somehow gotten the judge over your case to agree to try you as an adult. We're not sure how this happened, but it must have been something your court appointed attorney allowed, and we were not to know until you go to court."

"As an adult? What does that mean?" Jenny asked knowing it didn't sound good.

"It means, Jenny, if convicted you will spend more time behind bars and it won't be in a correction center with teens, but in prison with adult prisoners," Ruth said shaking her head as if she couldn't believe what was happening.

Fear rose in Jenny like a tidal wave. "What's the good news?" she asked.

"Our attorney has filed something to try and get it overturned, but we have to move forward as if the judge is going to let this stand," her father said. Jenny could tell by the worried look on his face that this was serious.

"So, what is the plan?" Jenny asked. "We're going to talk with your attorney, Jenny and you will tell him everything you know about what happened that night. It is imperative we have some type of defense to counter what they plan to throw at you."

"I can't, Dad," Jenny said.

"What do you mean you can't, Jenny?" He almost shouted. "We are talking about your future. What are you not telling us?"

"It's too late to say anything," Jenny replied.

"It's never too late to tell the truth," Dave said.

"This time it won't matter, because no one will believe me. You see, when Mr. Smith was yelling at the hospital and Anita was in hysterics saying it wasn't her - meaning it was me. Dad, I didn't say anything because I was shocked, she said that, but I would do anything to protect Anita. Now, they'll think I am trying to save myself. No one is going to believe me no matter what I say."

"How about letting us be the judge of that," Ruth said. "The one thing I do know is God will never honor or bless a lie. You know the difference between right and wrong, Jenny. Knowing what's right means little unless you do what's right. Telling the truth now is what's important."

"Even if it means hurting someone you care about," Dave told her. "You protecting Anita isn't in your best interest."

Jenny didn't reply but burst into tears. Miss Ruth put her arms around her and let her cry. Dave sat quietly. It was times like these he wishes his wife was here. She would know what to do to help their daughter.

When she finally stopped crying and raised her head, she was surprised to see her dad as calm as could be. "Will you go see the attorney with me and let's see what options he gives us for setting this right? This is no longer about protecting your friend from her father. It's about saving your life. You do understand that right?"

Jenny didn't say anything for a few minutes. "Dad, I need to think about this. Can we at least wait until Thursday to go see the attorney?"

"Jenny, I am telling you now, there is no thinking about this. Waiting until Thursday is not going to make it any easier. You have to tell all you know."

"Dad, I can't," Jenny whispers tears again running down her cheeks.

Dave Reynolds shook his head like he didn't understand and threw his hands up in the air before raking his hands through his hair. He stood up and paced across the room and looked out the window. His artificial foot seemed like a part of him now. He stood tall and straight, a military stance, with tension radiating from him.

Jenny didn't want to cause him more worry, but she still could not do what he asked. How did she explain to her dad she felt she had to protect her friend? "Dad it's going to be okay."

"No Jenny, it isn't going to be okay if you say nothing and are sent to prison for something, I don't believe you did," he declared. "That will never be okay."

"Dave, get an appointment for Thursday with her attorney," Miss Ruth said calmly.

Jenny and her dad both looked at Miss Ruth. Something passed between Ruth and him, and he nodded before walking over to the door. When the door closed Ruth went back to her quilt and sat down and went back to quilting.

Jenny had a little breathing room, but she knew this debate was far from over. *Lord, what do I do now? There's no going back on the mistakes I made that night. Please help me know what to do. I trust You, Lord and I am so grateful that you are my friend. Amen.*

Chapter Twenty

Jenny sat beside her dad listening to Christy Rivers sing *God Bless America*. When they first arrived, the program had already started but the words from *I Will Stand* rang out over the crowd. "Our values and valor still remain… So every time Old Glory is raised… I will stand for the stars… I will stand for the stripes… I will stand for the ones… who laid down their lives… So we can breathe in freedom… Every woman every man… For one nation under God… I will stand…"

Christy's beautiful voice held the audience enthralled. For more than an hour tribute song for Independence Day followed one after another. Each time the band on the stage was going to stop, the crowd asked for another song. It was long past time for the fireworks show, but no one seemed to mind.

Lots of families had chairs and blankets spread out across the parking lot listening to the performance. As Jenny listened, she realized Christy was singing words to a song she didn't recognize. She sang about how God had blessed America in the past because America had honored God. Now, people didn't seem to care so much about what God's Word said, they cared more about doing their own thing and what made them feel good. "God will not bless sin… He will not be mocked… America… America… God wants to bless America again… God wants to bless America again…" Jenny was so glad she lived in a land where she was free and where the people could still speak the name of God. It wasn't like that everywhere. Even in

America, the tide was turning away from God. There was no grantee America would always be free.

When the last word faded away, Christy bowed her head and said a brief prayer for the country. "Lord, we thank You for the blessings You have bestowed on this great country. We humbly pray Your guidance and protection. Help us to appreciate those who have paid the ultimate price for our freedom. As we celebrate on this July 4th let us forever be thankful to You God for what You have blessed us with and all the blessings You have in store for us in the future. Amen." After a brief pause, she said, "This will be the last song for the evening. It is a song written by Abigail Miller and it is named *America Bless God*. I hope you will listen to the words and say your thanks to the one who keeps us free."

The words flowing out over the audience held Jenny's attention. She told Christy about this song just a few days ago. "The privilege we hold… just to live in this great land… Do we recognize it as a gift… from God's almighty hand…? America, bless God… It is He that hath made us … and not us ourselves… Every blessing that we own… is a mercy from His throne… America, bless God…" Jenny felt tightness in her chest and tears formed in her eyes for the beautiful words and the truth she recognized from the first time she had heard it. While looking up lyrics for a gospel song, she had come across this one. She smiled. By the looks on the faces of the crowd, it certainly fit with the other songs that had been sung.

Jenny saw several of her old friends, but none of them came over to speak to her. A year ago, her life had been so different, and she knew by experience that overnight life can change. After Mark's death, many of her friends had stopped calling her friend and had stopped speaking to her. As she looked around earlier, she had noticed Tyler sitting with Anita on the second row of seats off to the left side of the stage. Thomas and Alma McCall were sitting close by with

Anita's grandmother. She was thankful that Tyler was talking to her, even riding with her for the first time yesterday as she scouted his grandfather's field. She couldn't help wondering what his relationship with Anita was. They both looked happy with their heads together and were laughing about something. She was glad Anita was getting out and about again, but she wondered what Mr. Smith and Willie would do when they found out. She knew they both were there somewhere in the crowd. Willie had caught Jenny's eye earlier but had quickly disappeared into the crowd moments later.

The music came to an end, and the crowd stood and applauded for several minutes before the announcer was able to tell them they would be lowering the lights for the firework show. It was only a few minutes later that the fireworks began, and it was a beautiful show, but she noticed her father didn't seem to be enjoying it much.

"Dad, would you like to go?" she asked.

"Yes, if you don't mind I would," he said getting up and taking his folding chair with him.

Jenny got up and took her chair and followed him as he worked his way out and away from the crowd. Soon the sound of the fireworks was all that was left. They were almost to her dad's truck when someone threw firecrackers under her dad's feet. He grabbed her and took her to the ground before she knew what was happening. His reaction was immediate. She could hear footsteps running away. There was also the sound of laughter fading but she didn't recognize who it was.

She had scraped her arm on the pavement, and it hurt badly, but she was more concerned with what was going on with her dad. It was several minutes before she was able to get up, but her dad wasn't responding to her. He seemed to be in some type of daze from the drama and she was frightened when he didn't say anything or seemed to be aware of where they were. She finally got him to get up, but he was not aware of where he was. Gathering up their chairs, she caught him by the arm and led him to his truck.

"It was just some kids playing with firecrackers, Dad," she told him. Still, he didn't say anything.

"Give me your keys," she said holding out her hand. He didn't hand her his keys, so she reached into his pocket and took them out. She pushed the unlock button and led him to the passage side. Once she got him in the truck, she buckled him in when he made no move to do it himself. Closing the door, she placed their chairs in the back and hurried around to the driver's side. She got in and adjusted the seat before fastening her own seat belt and cranking the engine. Driving them home was nerve-racking. She kept glancing over at him, but it was obvious the firecrackers caused a flashback. He was very quiet. She wished she knew what to do to help him. She noticed he was holding his head and leaning forward in his seat. *Was he in pain? What should she do?*

Jenny was getting worried by the time she pulled up in front of the old home place. She stopped the truck and turned the engine off. As she opened the door and hurried around the truck to the other side, she found him sitting, staring into space through the windshield. She was about to go knock on the front door to see if her dad's friend was there when he walked out on the front porch. Maybe he would know what to do for him.

She ran over to Bill and quietly asked, "I think my dad is in shock from the fireworks. Some kids threw fireworks under our feet after the program when we were on our way to the truck. I'm not sure what to do to help him."

"Let's try to get him inside," he said going over to her dad. She couldn't understand what he said to him, but she noticed her dad followed directions and got out of the truck. He still seemed to be in some type of trance and the man led him up the sidewalk to the front door.

When Jenny went to follow him inside, he stopped her. "I'll take it from here. I think it would be better if you took your dad's truck home tonight and came back in the morning. I'll give him one of his pills and put him to bed. It helps him sleep and he should be better in the morning."

"You will call me if he needs me?" she asked.

"He just needs rest, I'm sure he'll be better tomorrow." Jenny went back to the truck and cranked the engine. She turned the truck around and headed to Miss Ruth's house. She had never felt so helpless in her life. *Please Lord, be with Dad, let him be alright. I felt so helpless about what to do or say to help him. He has been so much better like he has a new lease on life. Please, Lord, You can make him well. You can heal him I know that you can.*

Chapter Twenty-One

fter sleeping very little the night before, Jenny was up early but not before Miss Ruth. She was glad she could share with her what had taken place the night before, wishing she knew what she could do to help her dad. Miss Ruth put medicine and a bandage on her arm where she scraped it when she hit the pavement.

"It should be good as new in a few days," Miss Ruth informed her.

"Miss Ruth, I was so afraid for Dad last night. I'm still worried how he will be this morning," Jenny admitted with a sad look on her face. "What am I going to do."

"Your dad needs you, Jenny," she said. "I don't know exactly what you plan to tell the lawyer today, but it's time you share the truth. You can't go to prison for something that was either an accident or someone else's fault. You understand what I'm saying?"

"After last night…" she hesitated. "I finally understand that I need to be here for Dad. I'll tell the truth and hope it's not too late."

"That is all we can ask, Honey," Ruth said.

"I'm going over to check on him this morning," she said as she gathered up her purse and keys. The sun had not come up as she walked out the door. There was enough light she could see how to get to her dad's truck. She knew she would be getting off to a late start with scouting her fields, but her dad was what was important now. When she arrived, he was sitting on the front porch with a cup of coffee in his hand. He seemed surprised to see her driving his truck and that she was there so early.

"What are you doing out this early?" he asked as she walked up on the porch.

"Hey, Dad, how are you feeling this morning?" Jenny asked, smiling as she noticed he seemed better than he did the last time she saw him.

"I feel fine, just can't remember how we got home last night. You must have driven us home. I'm guessing I had another one of my headaches. There isn't much I can do when I get one but take my meds and sleep it off."

"Do these headaches happen very often?" she asked.

"Often enough," he admitted smiling faintly.

She couldn't help but wonder what kind of answer that was? "I was glad Bill was here, and he knew what to do," Jenny replied not telling him what had actually happened since she wasn't sure what she should or shouldn't say. "Dad, I really would like to go with you to see your doctor sometime. I don't want to be in the position I was in last night not knowing what I needed to do to help you."

"I go again next month. We'll see," he answered gruffly.

Jenny remembered what was coming up next month and she didn't say anything else. It hit her again. She might be locked up by then. What help would she be to him should that happen?

"Do you remember anything about last night?" Jenny asked.

"I remember us going over to Hamburg and I remember the program, a really good one I might add, and then there is a blank. Did I get my headache, and we had to leave early?"

"We did leave early," Jenny agreed. She decided not to say anything else. Afraid he would get upset if he found out what had happened since he didn't remember. "Do you want to run me back to Miss Ruth's so I can get started on scouting my fields?"

"You're not scouting today," he answered. "We have an appointment to meet with the attorney at eleven this morning. When I talked to Thomas, he said not to worry about scouting. He has already told Tyler, so he isn't waiting for you. Would you like to come in and have some breakfast? I still know how to make pancakes. Of course, my new cook may already be working on something else."

"I would love to have breakfast," Jenny replied. She was so worried she left before eating and her stomach was rumbling.

"Then come on," he instructed getting out of the rocking chair, heading for the front door.

They walked into the kitchen just as Bill was putting plates on the table. "Looks like I need to add another plate," he said. Going over to the cabinet he got out another plate and silverware placing them on the table. "Sit down, breakfast is ready."

Jenny took a seat and heaped her plate with scrambled eggs, sausage, and biscuit with butter and grape jelly. She let Bill pour orange juice in her glass.

"This looks wonderful," she said. And it was. Jenny couldn't remember having a breakfast like this for a long time. When her grandmother was alive and well, she always cooked breakfast and said it was the most important meal of the day.

"Takes you back to some of grandma's breakfasts," her dad said smiling at her.

"Yes, I was just thinking that. I wish she could see what you have done with the house. She would be so happy you're doing better."

Jenny said as she smiled at him. "By the way, this is the best breakfast I have had in forever."

The phone on the kitchen wall rang. Her dad got up to answer it. She could only hear the conversation on this side, but he was telling someone they would be there by ten.

He walked back to the table and sat down. "We've got to be at the McCall's at ten this morning. I don't know what they need to see us about, but Thomas did sound like it was important we come before we go see your attorney."

"What do you think it is about?" Jenny questioned.

"Not sure but when you're finished, I am going to run you back to Ruth's place. I'll come back and get you in time to be at the McCall's by ten. We'll leave there and go straight to the attorneys' office. Ruth will have to go with us when I pick you up, we won't have time to go back to get her."

"I'm ready when you are," she said as she sipped the last of her orange juice and sat her glass back on the table. "Do I need to help clean up before we go?"

"No, go with Dave, I just need to load the dish washer and that will take only a few minutes," Bill said.

"Thanks, breakfast was delicious," she smiled. "I can see why the café is becoming so popular."

"I love to cook," he admitted.

"Maybe you can give me some lessons sometimes," Jenny said. "My grandmother taught me a lot, but I would love to be able to cook like you do. Especially desserts."

"That would be a pleasure," he added.

Dave came back into the room and asked, "You ready?"

"I am," she replied.

"Let's go then."

****

When they arrived at the McCall's a little before ten there were several cars and trucks already parked in the driveway. Jenny spotted Tyler standing near the front door. She couldn't help but wonder what was going on.

"Why are all these cars here? What do you think this is about, Dad?"

"Maybe about all those boys that were caught the other day," he answered. "I guess we will find out shortly."

Getting out of the truck she and Miss Ruth waited for him to come around before they started up the sidewalk to the porch.

Sheriff Bob Warren, the Sheriff came forward and shook her dad's hand. "Glad you're here. Come on in. We're waiting on Ted and Willie, and they should be here shortly."

"What's this all about, Bob?" Dave Reynolds questioned. "Be patience, it'll be worth your time," Bob said. "Jenny, Miss Ruth, come on in and we'll find you a place so you can get comfortable." He turned and led them into the house. Jenny gave Tyler a curious look as he stood holding the door open for them, but he just nodded at her as they passed by him.

Inside the door, Alma McCall came to greet them, giving Jenny a brief hug and showed them into the living room. "Come on in," she said.

Jenny was surprised that there was no one else in the living room. Where the people that all the vehicles parked out front were belonged to? They moved over to take a seat on the sofa.

A moment later the front door opened again, and Jenny could hear the voice she recognized as Ted Smiths.

"What's this all about, Bob? Why did you tell me to bring Willie over here now?" Then he rounded the corner and saw Jenny and her dad, and he said, "What are they doing here?"

"Ted, Willie, I need you to have a seat, and we'll get down to this meeting. You will understand shortly," Bob said pointing toward chairs.

A moment later, Louise Mayfield walked into the room and looked straight at Ted Smith. Ted jumped up, "You've got to be kidding me! What is she doing here?"

"Sit down, Ted and listen for once in your life," Louise said in a soft voice. "You're going to sit there and listen to what your daughter has to say, and you will not interfere. She's been living with this burden since the accident that killed her brother. If you love her, which I believe you do, you'll let her say what she needs to say."

Ted sank back into his chair and nodded his head. Louise walked across the hall to the den and opened the door. A moment later she returned to the living room with her arms around her granddaughter. She looked small and scared, but she held her head up and looked straight at her father and brother.

"Daddy, I need to tell you what happened the day of the accident. Mark's death was an accident and you blaming Jenny must stop."

"Look…" Ted started.

"Ted!" Louise cautioned with a warning in her voice.

He settled back into his chair and listened to his daughter.

"The morning of the dance, Mark took a key from your room and took liquor out of your cabinet. I'm not sure what he took, and I wish I had told you at the time. If I had he might still be alive," her voice broke and tears were running down her face. "Daddy, it was Mark who spiked the punch at the dance, I saw him do it. I didn't say anything. He thought it was funny and that no one would drink enough to really affect them. He was wrong. He was the one who drank too much."

Ted head went down, and Jenny felt sorry for him. He was crying now, and she couldn't hold her own tears when she saw the pain Anita was in. Had she done more harm than good by staying quiet? It was obvious that Anita had suffered because of what she knew and had not shared with anyone.

"Mark drank so much he had gotten silly and would have gotten in trouble if Jenny and I had not gotten him out of the gym that night. Jenny was driving his car when we left the dance. But Mark got sick, and we had to pull over for him twice. The second time Jenny got him back in the car, but he kept trying to climb over the seat. Finally, she got him to calm down and buckled in, so I got in the driver's seat, and she was in the back seat trying to keep him calm. We thought he had gone to sleep but suddenly, he unbuckled his seat belt and again tried to climb into the front seat saying he was going to drive. Jenny couldn't stop him, and he kicked me, and I lost control of the car. It is like it all happened in slow motion. We crossed into Tyler's lane and hit his car and back into our lane before going into the ditch and overturning. I don't know exactly what happened, only that after the car came to a stop I didn't know where Mark was. I don't know if I passed out for a minute or what, but I remember Jenny helping me get out of the car."

"Once she helped me out, she ran back to the car that we hit. I remember her calling out to me to come help her. I was looking for Mark, but I couldn't find him. I heard Tyler's car explode but I didn't know if Jenny was okay because I couldn't hear her after that. Later, there were sirens and flashing lights, and there were police and ambulances. I must have passed out again and the next thing I know I awoke in the hospital and Jenny was on a bed in the emergency room next to me. We were asking each other how each other were, and then Daddy you came in screaming about who killed your son. That was when I knew my brother was dead and I blamed Jenny because I was afraid to tell you the truth. Jenny was innocent and I was guilty. I was guilty of letting my brother die. If I had just told you. I can't forgive myself that I didn't tell you."

Ted walked over and took his daughter in his arms, and they cried together. Willie went to his grandmother, and she held him because he was also crying.

Jenny was crying as well, but the look on her dad's face was one of relief. Miss Ruth kept patting her on the shoulder and when she looked over at her there were tears in her eyes as well. "It's finally over, Jenny," Miss Ruth whispered. "God has answered our prayers."

It was over and Jenny could not describe the incredible feelings this knowledge gave her. She felt free for the first time in months. She would no longer have to worry about being locked up, or if her family would lose her grandparent's farm. Most important, she did not have to worry if Tyler would continue to hate her for his injuries. He would now know she had not been responsible for the accident.

Jenny's dad had tears in his eyes as he gathered his daughter into his arms and hugged her. "I thank God for answering our prayers," he said. "It is finally over."

Jenny looked at Anita. Their eyes met and Anita walked across the room to Jenny. Both girls hugged and cried all over again.

"I'm so sorry, Jenny," Anita said when she was finally able to speak.

"You'll always be my friend. I didn't mean to harm you by keeping quiet. I couldn't tell anyone because I thought I was protecting you," Jenny admitted.

"I know you were just trying to protect me, and I thank you for being my friend. I've lost Mark, but I don't want to lose you too."

"I'll always be your friend," Jenny whispered. "We're going to get through this."

"I've got to go with my grandmother and finish filling out a report that will have them dropping all charges against you," Anita said. I want to meet up in a day or two. We have so much to talk about.

Dave walked up and gave Jenny another hug. "Come on let's get out of here," he said. We're going to get your stuff from Miss Ruth's. It's time for you to come home."

"Miss Ruth …," Jenny started to say.

"I agree, as much as I love having you in my care, you need to go home with your dad," Ruth said with a smile on her face. "You can come over to visit any time you want."

As they left Jenny looked around for Tyler, but she did not see him.

Chapter Twenty-Two

Two days later Jenny felt like she was involved in a revolving door at her dad's place. Sheriff Bob Warren had been out to their place four times. Each time he came by it was with a different boy and his parents. The boy would come in and offer an admission of guilt for the part they had played in damaging her jeep and for frightening her. Their parents would also apologize and express regret for their sons' behavior. They would then promise it would never happen again.

Jenny accepted their apologies but felt that she would never feel quite the same way about any of them again. It wasn't that she couldn't forgive them. It was because it seemed to her, they each had been too easily led astray. They were too ready to lay all the blame on Willie, who was their friend. He was really hurting over losing his brother. Why had they not tried to talk him out of his revenge?

The fact that they were to serve sixty hours doing community service made it a little better. They also had to share the cost of having her jeep repaired.

The last visit was the one that Jenny wished she could avoid altogether. Ted Smith and Willie were the last to come by. She had no idea how she was going to respond to them.

"They will be here in a few minutes, Jenny," Bob said as he looked at his watch. "I'm sure they will say they're sorry. I also know they did a lot of damage to you with all that you had to go through by the things they did and said. Let them know how you're feeling."

He had just finished speaking when they saw a black club cab Chevy truck pulled up and park.

"Ted, Willie, I'm glad you decided to come by today," Bob said.

Ted didn't say anything. It was obvious he didn't want to be there. Jenny had already figured out that each of the boys was required to apologize as part of their punishment. She sat with her dad on the porch while the sheriff stood to the side and let Willie go first.

He came over to them. "Jenny, I want you to know I'm sorry for the way I've treated you," he said. "I hope that one day you might be able to forgive me for all the trouble I caused you."

"Willie, I've kept in mind how much you were hurting and how much you loved your brother. I know you were getting back at the one you thought took him from you. You were so wrong with how you talked to me and treated me. Not only that, but you also convinced your friends to help you. I don't understand why you're such a bully. I hope you'll work on getting help for that."

"Look, I said I was sorry," he said.

"Yes, you did. I hope you really mean it and have learned something. I also hope one day I can forgive you," Jenny said.

Ted came over and put his hand on his son's shoulder. "Jenny, my son said he was sorry. I thought you were a Christian and would forgive him."

"Mr. Smith, you are as guilty as Willie. He has watched you model for him and he just doing what he was seeing you do."

"I'll admit I've been a bully, and I've said and done some pretty terrible things as well. We got all charges dropped. Bob has the taped confession Anita gave and it's obvious that neither of you were responsible for the accident that took my son's life. If anyone was at fault it was Mark. He knew better than to take liquor and spike the punch. He did it anyway. Your name is cleared of any wrong doing."

"So, the slate should just be wiped clean and all forgiven?" Jenny didn't know what to say. She was angry they were standing there saying they were sorry, and she was just supposed to say I forgive you. Ted was going to take their home and now acted like he hadn't done anything wrong. She found herself saying. "I'm so sorry for your loss, Mr. Smith. I'm glad you know that it was an accident. You need to really think about what you did in the name of grief. You were out to see someone pay for your son's death. There is no excuse for your behavior toward your own daughter."

"Now look here, I didn't come over here to be lectured by you," Ted said.

There it was, even when he was saying he was sorry, he still had the attitude that he really wasn't in the wrong. It was there in his voice and Jenny couldn't help but wonder if either of them was really sorry for all that had happened.

"If you're really sorry, I accept your apology," Jenny finally said.

Ted laughed as he shook his head. "How will you ever know if we are sincere or not?" Ted asked. "You have your doubts, I can hear them in your voice."

"You're right, I doubt you're sincere."

"We said we're sorry," Willie replied. "You can take it or leave it! It doesn't matter to me."

"And that, Willie, is what I'm talking about. Would you be here today if it wasn't a requirement for the trouble you're in?"

Willie stared at her for a moment before saying, "No!"

"Willie, I told you…" Ted started to say.

"It doesn't matter, Mr. Smith," Jenny said. "I choose to forgive you both for myself. You see, I don't like these feelings of distrust and anger that I have because of your actions. With God's help I forgive you, because it's what I know He wants me to do."

"You sound so self-righteous." Ted laughed.

"Call it whatever you like," Jenny said. None of us can undo the past but we can choose how to react in the future. My prayer is that you both have learned something from this experience and will choose to do what is right in the future. Once the words were out of her mouth, she felt like a weight had been lifted from her shoulders and she smiled at them.

"We'll be going," Ted said. He and his son walked away.

"Are you all right, Jenny?" Bob asked.

"I am."

"I'm glad you said what you did today to those two. I'm not sure it will sink in, but God does work in ways we can't see sometimes," Bob said.

"I have been praying on how to respond to them. It all depended on how and what they had to say."

"You handled it well," Dave said.

"I agree and I think I can be on my way, too," Bob said.

"Thanks for being here today, Bob," Dave said as he shook hands with his friend.

"Glad this is over, and we can move forward."

Dave sat back down in the rocker beside his daughter. "So, you chose to forgive them."

"I realized as soon as they started to speak, I don't think they really meant it when they said they were sorry. They didn't sound sincere. Then I knew it doesn't matter what I think. What does matter is what God knows."

"That is true."

"He knows my heart. He knows I do not want to live with hate inside me."

"I'm glad, Jenny," Dave said. "You sound a lot like your grandma. She would have been very proud of you today. Just like I am."

Jenny smiled at her father's words. He was proud of her. She knew the Smith's had been suffering for the past few months, their lives on hold waiting on a court date that now would never come. How could she not say she forgave them? She knew Mr. Smith would continue to endure pain at the loss of his son for the rest of his life. The fact it was his liquor Mark had taken would add to that burden. Thank God, it was finally over. Maybe life could finally get back to normal. Whatever normal was.

Chapter Twenty-Three

A nita and Jenny visit Mark's grave together two days later after the Sunday morning service. The preacher had preached a good sermon on loving your neighbor and the miracle that God had in store for those who loved Him. He reminded the congregation what a friend they each had in Jesus. A true friend who would lay down His life for all who would place their faith in Him. The grace of God will change hearts and lives only if people will accept the gift that Jesus died to give each person who had ever lived. He quoted the words Jesus said, "I am the resurrection and the life. Whoever believes in me, though he dies, yet shall he live."

They each placed yellow roses on Mark's grave. Then they spent a quiet moment saying a silent prayer for brother and friend. Anita was the first to speak, "I want to thank God today for my brother and because we both put our faith in Jesus Christ as Savior and Lord, I know I will see him again in heaven someday."

"I want to thank God today that I had a chance to have you as a good friend Mark Smith and that I will see you again one day in heaven as well," Jenny said following her friend example. "I want to also thank God today that I have a friend like Anita and that God has brought her back into my life as a true friend."

A few minutes later they walked back to the church where they had left their cars, they paused in the shade of an old oak tree. Anita turned to Jenny and said, "You should know that Tyler really went to bat for you when he learned it wasn't me who pulled him from his car. He listened to me when I needed someone to talk to. He was the one who told me I had to tell the truth about that night. I would say he is what a true friend is, and I think you are very fortunate to have him as your friend."

"You are telling me this because…" Jenny said with eyes filled with tears and a smile on her face. "I really like him."

"He really cares about you too Jenny," Anita replied.

"You're sure about that?" Jenny asked. For years she had thought about Tyler McCall, first with a young girl crush, and in the last few weeks as a maturing young woman who could really grow to love the young man he was. She loved the fact that he loved God and had shared his testimony with her more than once. She loved the fact that he had been a friend when she needed one the most. She wasn't sure what plans God had for her in the future, but she was hopeful that it would include a relationship with Tyler.

When they returned to the church parking lot most of the people had already left. Anita left Jenny to go and get in her car. Tyler was standing beside her jeep as she walked over to it.

"Any chance you would give a guy a ride home?" He asks with a smug smile on his face.

"That depends," she answered with a grin.

"On what?" he asked.

"If he was going to supply lunch?" She laughed. "It's in the picnic basket already in your jeep. I thought we might go have a picnic out at our favorite place," he told her. "There are cinnamon rolls in there somewhere and I know how much you like your cinnamon rolls."

"What are we waiting on kind sir, I am starving."

Tyler got in the passenger seat and Jenny got in the driver's seat and cranked it up. After they both buckled seatbelts, she drove to the old McDonald's place. There was a for sale sign on the property the last time they were there. The sign was missing, and she couldn't help but wonder if they would be able to use the pond as a picnic area for much longer.

"Do you think someone has purchased it?" She asked when they came to a stop at the end of the lane that led to the pond.

"I know it's sold," Tyler said.

"Really! Do you know who bought it?"

"Does it matter?" He asked.

"Well, it could mean that we'll be trespassing on the property, and someone might not want us to be on it in the future."

"Let's just enjoy today and we'll let tomorrow take care of itself."

"You aren't going to tell me who purchased it?"

"Maybe later," he answered. "Let's eat. I'm hungry."

They enjoyed the lunch and the refreshing breeze that kept it from being too hot in the shade. Jenny looked over at Tyler who sat relaxed on the blanket and was staring at her. "Why did you let everyone think you were at fault, Jenny?" Tyler asked, taking her hand when she would have moved away from him.

"Why not?" Jenny answered. "You've seen for yourself what Anita's dad was like. He was very frightening the night that Mark died. Anita was in so much pain, I just couldn't correct what she said."

"Did you think no one would ever know?"

She swallowed biting down on her lips. For the first time she thought about the burden she had accepted in the place of her friend.

At the time she did it to protect Anita when her dad had been at the hospital shouting at them.

"There is a verse in the *Bible* that says, Greater love hath no man than this, that a man lay down his life for his friends. I'm no hero Tyler, but at that moment I would have given anything to help her."

"Yeah, I know the verse, think it's John 15:13," Tyler said.

"At the time I just didn't correct them when she said I was the one driving," Jenny added. "Then Anita didn't say anything different in the following days, I think the way her dad was acting she was afraid to tell him. Of course, I was the one driving when we left the school heading home. So, everyone assumed I was the one behind the wheel when the wreck happened. We had to stop more than once for Mark to be sick. The last time Mark wanted Anita to drive."

"Would you have told the truth if Anita hadn't spoken up?"

"After a while, it was just too late to say anything. No one would have believed me if I had said I wasn't driving. They would think I was just trying to get out of going to jail.""So, you were going to give up your freedom for your friend?" Tyler said in a soft voice. He placed his fingers under her chin, so she was looking him in the eye.

"Then you came alone asking too many questions," she said a mixture of pain and regret in her gaze.

"I don't know how you got me out of my car that night, but I know you saved my life. Once I knew that, there was no way that I would let you be locked up for something you didn't do. I know you told me once that you would not talk about that night. Now, can you tell me what really happened? I know Anita was the one driving I still don't know all of it."

"Mark was the one who caused the accident. We thought he had passed out and suddenly, he unbuckled his seatbelt and tried to climb into the front seat. I was trying to stop him, but I couldn't, and he hit Anita in the head and arm and caused her to lose control of the car. It crossed into your lane and hit you and then back into our lane before going into the ditch and overturning. I really don't know how I got out, but once I helped Anita out, I ran back to see if you were okay. Of course, you were unconscious, but I managed to get you out and dragged you away from your car. Your car explored and I must have passed out before help got there."

"Were you drinking that night?" Tyler asked.

"I don't drink alcohol, but Anita said Mark spiked the punch. I didn't know it was spiked and no one said anything. It seems Anita knew but didn't tell me. Since it was a school function, I doubt anyone would have admitted knowing anything because they would have gotten in trouble. After my blood test showed alcohol in my blood stream, I know that's the only way I could have tested positive to drinking alcohol that night.""All this time I thought you were a drunk driver who caused the wreck."

"I know," Jenny said.

"I've said this before, but I am saying it again, I'm sorry for the way I treated you," Tyler said. "Do you think you might someday forgive me?"

Jenny smiled. "Someone once told me to be a true friend we have to be willing to forgive those who hurt us."

Tyler laughed, "That was a smart someone."

"Tyler McCall, you have been a true friend to me. I will never forget what you did to help set all this straight. I would love to continue being your friend in the future," Jenny said a smile on her face that was finally free of worries about keeping secrets that could harm someone else.

"I'll be around the rest of the summer, but I plan to go back to the University of Arkansas this fall and become a basketball coach. I might not be able to play the game, but that doesn't mean I can't help others become good players. My coach has already said he will mentor me and who knows, I may someday coach at the college level. God knows the plans He has for me. I don't have to know all of it yet."

"I believe you can do anything you set your mind to Tyler McCall," Jenny said as she smiled at her friend.

"Well, I've been determined to do this for a while," he said as he placed his fingers under her chin to tilt her face up. She saw a promise in his eyes that had her heart pounding in her chest before she closed her eyes because she knew he was finally going to kiss her.

www.ingramcontent.com/pod-product-compliance
Lightning Source LLC
Chambersburg PA
CBHW051114050726
47592CB00002B/820